FACING AND OVERCOMING
ADVERSITY

Copyright © 2026 by Martin Freeman.

ISBN (eBook/Kindle): 978-1-968012-92-2

ISBN (Paperback): 978-1-968012-93-9

ISBN (Hardcover): 978-1-968012-94-6

Library Of Congress Catalog Card Number: 2026905372

All rights reserved. No part of this book may be reproduced or transmitted in any form or by any means, electronic or mechanical, including photocopying, recording, or by any information storage and retrieval system without express written permission from the author, except in the case of brief quotations embodied in critical reviews and certain other noncommercial uses permitted by copyright law.

Published in the United States of America by Lynx Publishers.

FACING AND OVERCOMING ADVERSITY

A STRATEGIC APPROACH TO BUILDING K-12 RESILIENT STUDENTS

MARTIN FREEMAN

This book is dedicated to the incredible teachers, administrators, support staff, students, and families of the Youngstown City School District. Your resilience, love, courage, compassion, and unwavering belief in what's possible for our students make all the difference.

TABLE OF CONTENTS

Foreword	vi
Preface	xv
Introduction	18
Chapter 1 – The Meaning of Resilience	20
Chapter 2 – Why the Science of Resilience Matters	27
Chapter 3 – The Nature and Nurture of Resilience	33
Chapter 4 – Why Is Resilience Important	39
Chapter 5 – The Foundations of Resilience	47
Chapter 6 – Identifying and Understanding Risk and Protective Factors	54
Chapter 7 – Adversity as A Teacher: Understanding How Adversity Shapes Resilience	64
Chapter 8 – Educator Resilience: The Heartbeat of a Thriving School	68
Chapter 9 – Resilience as a necessity in Today's Educational Climate	76
Chapter 10 – Teaching Student's to Name Their Feelings and Needs	82
Chapter 11 – Creating A Resilient Classroom Environment	87
Chapter 12 – What Resilient Students Do Differently: Profiles, Patterns, and Practices	95
Chapter 13 – Rewriting the Story: Teaching Students to Challenge False Narratives	100
Chapter 14 – Growth Mindset and How It Influences Resilience	105
Chapter 15 – Hope: Teaching Students to See Possibility	110
Chapter 16 – From Struggle to Strength: How Students Grow Beyond Adversity	122
Chapter 17 – The Need for Resilience-Based Interventions for Students	129
Chapter 18 – Profiles in Resilience	135
Acknowledgements	151
About the Author	152
References	153

FOREWORD

"Resilience is not a construct, I encountered first in research or professional learning. It is something I learned through experience; through challenge, responsibility, and the weight of leading in moments where outcomes mattered deeply for children, families, and communities.

My journey in education, from the classroom to district leadership, has been shaped by adversity and sustained by purpose. In urban education especially, resilience is not a supplemental skill. It is foundational. That is precisely why Facing and Overcoming Life's Adversities: A Strategic Approach to Building K–12 Resilient Students is both timely and necessary.

Dr. Martin Freeman's work stands at the intersection of scholarship, practice, and moral leadership. He approaches resilience not as an abstract psychological concept, but as a systemic responsibility of schools ;especially those serving students and communities that have historically carried the greatest burden of inequity. His scholarship is rigorous, grounded in research, and deeply informed by the realities of K–12 education. Just as importantly, his writing reflects a profound respect for educators and students whose lived experiences often go unrecognized in policy conversations.

On a personal level, Dr. Freeman's work resonates with me because it mirrors what I have come to understand through years of service in urban school systems: resilience is built, sustained, and either strengthened or eroded by the systems we design. His work affirms that resilience is not about asking students and educators to endure hardship in silence, nor is it about celebrating struggle for struggle's sake. Instead, it is about transforming conditions so that adversity becomes a catalyst for growth rather than a barrier to opportunity. Urban education demands this level of clarity.

In districts like Youngstown, educators are called to do more than deliver curriculum. They are asked to lead, to heal, to stabilize, and to believe—often in the face of generational trauma, economic instability, staffing shortages, and shifting policy demands. Dr. Freeman names these realities honestly, without deficit framing. He situates resilience within the broader context of systems change, emphasizing that sustainable improvement requires intentional alignment of culture, leadership, instruction, and well-being.

What distinguishes Dr. Freeman's contribution is his insistence that resilience must be embedded into the fabric of school improvement efforts. His work challenges leaders to move beyond compliance-driven reform and toward coherent systems that prioritize psychological safety, professional competence, meaningful relationships, and shared purpose. This perspective aligns deeply with continuous improvement models and with the work of districts committed to long-term transformation rather than short-term fixes.

As Superintendent, I have seen firsthand that when resilience is treated as a system-level priority, outcomes change. Educators are more likely to remain in the profession. School leaders are better equipped to navigate complexity. Students experience greater consistency, trust, and opportunity. Dr. Freeman provides the field with a framework that validates these truths while offering practical strategies for implementation across diverse educational contexts.

This book also reflects a deep understanding of leadership. Dr. Freeman recognizes that educator resilience is inseparable from leadership practice. Principals and district leaders do not merely manage systems; they shape the emotional and relational climate in which teaching and learning occurs. His emphasis on purpose, connection, competence, and well-being speaks directly to the kind of leadership required to transform urban schools into places of stability, hope, and high expectation.

I am particularly honored that this book is dedicated to the educators, students, and families of the Youngstown City School District. Their resilience is not theoretical. It is lived daily in classrooms, hallways, and communities striving for renewal.

My hope is that this book serves as both a guide and a call to action. A guide for educators seeking to better support students facing adversity. A call to action for leaders and policymakers to build systems worthy of the people they serve. Dr. Freeman has given the field a work that is intellectually sound, deeply human, and urgently relevant.

When resilience is understood as a shared responsibility and embedded within systems, schools do more than improve; they transform. And in urban education, transformation is not optional. It is imperative."

By Jeremy J. Batchelor, M.S. Ed., ePHCLE, pHCLE
Superintendent, Youngstown City School District

There are certain people whose presence immediately puts others at ease—people whose work is not defined by a title, but by the way they consistently show up for others. Dr. Martin Freeman is one of those people. First and foremost, he is a genuinely good human being. His insight, compassion, and unwavering commitment to people's well-being have made him a trusted advocate for families, staff, and students throughout the Youngstown City School District.

MARTIN FREEMAN

In his role as Ombudsman, Dr. Freeman serves as a vital bridge between families, educators, and the school system. Before this role, his work as the McKinney-Vento Liaison reflected the very heart of service—ensuring that our most vulnerable students had access to necessities, dignity, and stability while helping families navigate incredibly difficult circumstances. His work has always centered on care, advocacy, and equity, and that commitment continues to define his leadership today.

Anyone who knows Dr. Freeman knows that his professionalism is matched by his humanity. When he walks into a school, he does not rush past people; he greets them. He stops. He listens. He checks in—not because he has to, but because he genuinely cares. At Rayen Early College Middle School, his visits are always welcome. He makes it a point to say hello to everyone in the main office and to any staff member or student he encounters along the way. His cheerful greetings and sincere concern leave people feeling seen and valued. And if you know him well, you also know his love for Cleveland sports—a passion he eagerly shares, often calling my husband for animated conversations that reflect his joy in connection just as much as the game itself.

Chapter 8, *Educator Resilience: The Heartbeat of a Thriving School*, speaks powerfully to the lived reality of educators in the Youngstown City School District. Teaching here—like in many urban districts—requires far more than content knowledge. It demands emotional strength, adaptability, compassion, and a deep sense of purpose. Our educators carry academic expectations while also supporting students through trauma, uncertainty, and challenges that extend beyond the classroom walls. This chapter affirms what we know to be true: resilience is not about perfection or endurance alone; it is about sustaining hope, purpose, and connection in the midst of complexity.

FACING AND OVERCOMING ADVERSITY

Doc's book puts emphasis on purpose, competence, connection, and well-being mirrors what I see daily in our schools. Purpose anchors our educators to their "why"—the belief that their work matters and that every child deserves opportunity. Competence gives them the confidence to adapt and respond to ever-changing needs. Connection sustains them through collaboration, shared problem-solving, and supportive leadership. And well-being reminds us that caring for educators is not optional; it is essential if we expect them to care for others.

In Youngstown City Schools, we proudly call our students **scholars**. That word is intentional. It reflects what we believe about our students and what we see in them every day. I believe deeply in our scholars—their brilliance, their resilience, and their capacity for success. I witness countless successes: scholars achieving academic milestones, discovering their voices, setting goals for the future, and overcoming obstacles with determination and pride. These moments of success are fueled by resilient educators who create environments where scholars feel safe, supported, challenged, and inspired.

This chapter reminds us that when educators are supported, students thrive. Resilient educators model perseverance, emotional regulation, and hope—skills our scholars absorb and carry with them. In a district like Youngstown, resilience is not an abstract concept; it is a shared practice and a collective strength. It lives in our classrooms, our relationships, and our unwavering commitment to our scholars' success.

Dr. Freeman's leadership embodies the very principles outlined in this book. His advocacy, compassion, and steady presence reinforce the systems and relationships that allow resilience to flourish. He reminds us that schools succeed not only through policies and programs, but through people—people who care deeply, lead with integrity, and believe in the promise of every child.

This work is a testament to the power of resilience, community, and belief. It honors the educators who continue to show up, the scholars who continue to strive, and the leaders—like Dr. Martin Freeman—who ensure that humanity remains at the center of education.

Dr. Maureen E. Donofrio, Ed. D.
Principal
Youngstown Rayen Early College Middle School
Youngstown City School District

"As the director of Choffin Career and Technical Center in Youngstown, Ohio. I have spent the last nine years leading a school that serves students who often carry significant adversity, including economic hardship, family instability, trauma, and the lingering effects of a global pandemic. Before coming to Youngstown, I served five years in urban education as a high school administrator in Rockford, Illinois. Across both communities, I have witnessed firsthand how resilience is not an abstract ideal but a necessity for our students, our educators, and ourselves.

At Choffin, we have built a strong culture around three very clear goals: graduate on time, earn industry certifications, and be career and college ready. These goals are more than metrics on a school report card, they are lifelines of opportunity for our students. Through our many internal initiatives for success including built in milestone achievements, our expanded support for academics with a lens in CTE, pre-apprenticeships and career placements, and a data tracking system that enables us to create individualized success plans for each of our students, we remove barriers and open up multiple pathways to graduation and lifelong success. These efforts have allowed our students to earn a high school diploma at our school at a much higher rate than other buildings in our district and the highest among all urban career and technical centers in Ohio.

We have earned a five-star rating on the Ohio Report Card for two consecutive years and remain on track for a third year. None of this would be possible without resilient educators, administrators, and support staff who show up every day ready to guide, mentor, and believe in our students. This book speaks directly to the reality we live at Choffin, and chapter 8 especially resonates, as it articulates what I witness daily; resilient staff remaining calm in chaos, having hope in uncertainty, and perseverance through setbacks. When our staff are grounded in purpose, supported by connection, confident in their competence, and intentional in their work, they create the stable environments our students need to thrive and succeed.

This work is forged on the front lines and is dedicated to the administrators, educators, support staff, students, and families of the Youngstown City School District and the districts that resemble us. To my fellow urban school leaders and staff: this book offers a practical, evidence-informed framework to build resilience in both our students and ourselves. Read it, share it with your teams, and put its strategies into action. Our young people are counting on us. It is an honor and privilege to introduce this essential book."

MARTIN FREEMAN

Dr. Michael Saville, Ed.D.
Director
Choffin Career and Technical Center
Youngstown City School District

As I reflect on the chapters in this book, I can say that as a teacher it is an opportunity to reward them for their resiliency and understand that what they do on a daily basis is not easy and not to be taken for granted. This book reminds me of the strength, love and determination that teachers display every day as they enter into a classroom and leave the building for the day. This book reminds me of what it means to face adversity and bounce back. It reminds me of how teachers work with their students and together they face trauma, challenges and stress but they use their inner strength to overcome these barriers.

I wish I had this book when I was teaching as it would have provided me with what Dr. Martin Freeman references throughout the book on how resilience emerges at the intersection of purpose, competence, connection and well-being. It shows us the reasons we do what we do and why it is important to stay steadfast regardless of what comes our way as an educator. It shows us that resiliency is what builds our confidence within ourselves so we can be better for our students in the classroom. As you continue to read this book, you will also learn the importance of connection and the importance of one's well-being is self-care and self-reflection.

I wish I had this book when I started as an administrator because it would have provided me a clearer understanding on what it means to be resilient and what to look for in teachers. As an administrator, you too want to be resilient but you also want to have the tools to identify resilience among others. Dr.

FACING AND OVERCOMING ADVERSITY

Freeman gives you these tools with the understanding that "resilience is not simply what helps us survive: it's what teaches us how to live fully, love deeply, and lead courageously." It is the capacity to withstand and recover. Resiliency is the importance of surviving, taking a stand and believing in yourself and others. In this book, Dr. Freeman provides you with a better understanding of resilience and how to practice it throughout the classroom. As a teacher it provides you the tools needed to maintain your own resilience and also build the resiliency of our students. It is a great read that will demonstrate for educators how to cope and through these coping strategies how it will affect our students. Afterall, isn't the goal to produce resilient students?

I know Dr Freeman to be a man of great character and an upstanding leader. He not only researches but he shares real life experiences that support his writings such as building resilient teachers and students. Dr. Freeman's passion shows in this book. His experience as a social worker, pastor, and educator grants him the confidence to speak first hand on what resilient teachers look like in a school district and the power in their words and actions to bring resiliency among students. This book captures the authors' insight and provides each of you with both guidance, direction and inspiration.

Kelly D. Washington, Ph.D.
Principal/Adjunct Professor
Taft Elementary
Youngstown City School District

PREFACE

Have you ever been in a dark place? You were down for the count, Isolated, no hope. You conceptualized, internalized, even verbalized the failure, crisis, adversity you were going through? You were dismayed and couldn't see beyond what you were experiencing but with time, in time you, and through time you began to heal, bounce back, and recover. That's the reality for many children navigating adversity.

In every classroom, hallway, playground, and office, there are stories of students who wake up each day carrying more than backpacks. Many come with grief, instability, trauma, pressure, and invisible battles that shape how they learn, behave, and see their future. Yet, time and again, we also see something powerful emerge—students who discover strength, connection, and hope even in the midst of challenge. This book, Facing and Overcoming Adversity: A Strategic Approach to Building K–12 Resilient Students, was written for the educators, leaders, and caring adults who believe that resilience is not accidental; that it can be nurtured, taught, and strengthened with intentional practice.

Trauma, struggle, setbacks, disappointment, failure, challenge, and grief are all part of the human experience but so is resilience. Many of our children have experienced, are experiencing, or will experience feeling down and out, depressed, dejected, defeated? Many of them, unable to verbalize are internally asking themselves, when will the hurt, pain, and suffering end? How much longer do I have to endure the misery, and the suffocating thoughts that render me discouraged, even disconnected? They ask themselves, can I, will I get through this dark time in my life?

Resilience is not about eliminating hardship; it is about equipping students with the inner resources, external support, and learning environments that help them adapt, heal, and thrive. Schools are uniquely positioned to do this work. They are more than academic institutions—they are centers of belonging, safety, restoration, and human growth. This book provides a practical, research-informed roadmap to help school communities cultivate resilience in purposeful, compassionate, and strategic ways.

Resilience isn't just about "bouncing back," it's significant in that it's about growing through challenges, developing emotional strength, and learning that setbacks don't define us. Resilience, for children, develop throughout their lives and is attained by what they observe and imitate. It's built through relationships, support, and the environments we create for them, especially educators.

We tend to idealize childhood as a carefree time, but youth alone doesn't offer a shield against the emotional hurts, challenges, and trauma many of our children face. Our children are asked to deal with problems ranging from adapting to a new classroom, online schooling, struggles at home and deadly encounters in their neighborhoods, communities, and city streets. Also, they face the uncertainties that are part of growing up in a complex world. How many of you reading this book know that childhood can be anything but carefree? The ability to thrive despite these challenges arises from the skills of learning to be resilient. Make no mistake, ups and downs, changes and turnarounds are part of life but in the long run, those challenges can help our children become stronger and teach them valuable lessons.

In this book we're going to explore how we, as an educational system can foster resilience, helping children not just survive adversity but thrive regardless of it. I'm confident the strategies provided will unlock resilience in ways that will engage you, allowing you to glean and grasp from these strategies, then teaching and helping our children practically apply them to their lives.

My hope is that these pages affirm what educators already know in their hearts: that every student has capacity, potential, and worth—and with the right systems, relationships, and supports, they can rise beyond adversity and build lives anchored in strength, hope, and possibility.

FACING AND OVERCOMING ADVERSITY

INTRODUCTION

Every day, in classrooms, hallways, and homes across our communities, students are fighting battles we cannot always see. Some carry the weight of fractured families, silent trauma, unmet needs, academic pressure, or environments that challenge their sense of safety and belonging. Despite these obstacles something remarkable continues to rise within them: It's called resilience.

Resilience is not the absence of hardship; it is the courage to stand in the midst of it. It is the quiet determination of a student who shows up to school even when life looks bleak, and they feel overwhelmed. It is the strength of a student who refuses to let failure define them. It is the hope that emerges in young people who choose growth instead of giving up.

Students are not shaped by the adversity itself, but by the support, skills, and belief systems that help them push through it. Resilience grows when caring adults' (parents, guardians, teachers, social workers, coaches) step in, when schools create safe spaces, and when students learn that their story is not limited by their struggle, and in fact, has yet to be told. What they face may challenge them but it doesn't and must not defeat them.

This generation of students today, must rise above circumstances that often breaks others. When we teach them how to harness resilience, we're not just helping them survive difficult moments we're empowering them to transform adversity into strength, struggle into wisdom, and obstacles into opportunities. Their resilience is not just a skill; it is their gateway to hope, healing, and a future filled with possibility.

Resilience is not born in the peaceful setting of tranquility, but forged in the fires of adversity. It's in the struggle, not the stillness, that strength takes place—it is discovered in the storms of life. It does not call out its presence; it discloses itself through the moments when we choose to rise again, when we encourage ourselves to get up one more time. Resilience is the human spirit's declaration that I've been broken but not defeated, and weary does not mean I'm done.

In classrooms, communities, and homes, we see resilience every day. It's the teacher who shows up for students after facing their own losses. It's the student who keeps believing that tomorrow can be better than today. It's the parent who chooses to love their child with hope, even when life feels uncertain.

This book is about that kind of strength—the kind that grows quietly beneath the surface. It's about how adversity can become the soil where purpose takes root, how hope can be practiced, and how healing can become a way of life.

Resilience is not simply what helps us survive; it's what teaches us how to live fully, love deeply, and lead courageously. Resilience teaches us that adversity does not define us—it develops us. It reveals that strength is often born out of struggle and that setbacks, while painful, can become powerful turning points. Through resilience, we learn that we are far more capable than we ever imagined, that asking for help is an act of courage, and that hope can carry us through even the darkest seasons. Resilience shows us how to adapt when life shifts, how to regulate our emotions when they feel overwhelming, and how to hold on to purpose when challenges try to distract us. Most of all, resilience reminds us that healing is possible—that our past may shape us, but it does not have to limit our future.

My hope is that as you turn these pages, you'll not only learn about resilience but you'll begin to see it in yourself.

Chapter 1 – The Meaning of Resilience

When tackling this question what is resilience, I knew from the onset it would be a daunting challenge. The field of resilience research is not short on inquiry, and defining resilience comes with a plethora of explanations. When discussing resilience, one must consider

(1) how should resilience be defined,

(2) what are the critical factors of resilience,

(3) how does the science of resilience inform research today,

(4) and how can we practically apply resilience to everyday living.

Those in the field of research today stand on the shoulders of giants, meaning those who've trod the path of discovery and who worked tirelessly to provide a framework that sill helps us grasp the very meaning of the term resilience today. Norman Germezy, Emmy Werner, Michael Rutter, and Ann Masten (still living) were and are the pioneers of resilience research. Their work focused on understanding how children coped with adversity and were able to thrive despite their difficult circumstances.

I trust that, reading this book, you will agree that resilience is an intricate word that can be defined differently in the context of individuals, families, organizations, societies, and cultures. The research and science of resilience continues to build as now fields of neuroscience, mental health, medicine, psychology, and sociology have emerged and engaged in the quest to bring understanding to this word.

The word resilient is the new "buzz," word today. Resilience is a word being used across disciplines, sectors and professions. You will hear the word used in politics, sports, even in the halls of academia. Though it is a word frequently being used, it is often used out of context. When asked what resilience means, the answer varies from vague to often misunderstood, depending on who you ask, and in what setting it is being used.

Psychologist, from the 1970's, until present day have defined resilience in various ways: Garmezy defined resilience as, "Not necessarily impervious to stress. Rather, resilience is designed to reflect the capacity for recovery and maintained adaptive behavior that may follow initial retreat or incapacity upon initiating a stressful event" (Garmezy, 1991a).

Masten defined resilience as, "The capacity of a dynamic system to adapt successfully to disturbances that threaten system function, viability, or future development of the system" (Ann Masten, 2014).

Rutter defined resilience as, "An interactive concept that is concerned with the combination of serious risk experiences and a relatively positive psychological outcome despite those experiences" (Rutter, 2006).

Werner defined resilience as, "The capacity [of individuals] to cope effectively with the internal stresses of their vulnerabilities (labile patterns of autonomic reactivity, developmental imbalances, unusual sensitivities) and external stresses (illness, major losses, and dissolution of the family)" (Werner, 1982).

Many others have contributed definitions and explanations of resilience however, the most clear, concise, and poignant definition of resilience, in my opinion, is "The ability to weather and recover from adversity" (Southwick et al. 2014). The aforementioned definition is simple, yet profound.

We must recognize that adversity is multifaceted and in that, regarding children we could include child abuse, exposure to neighborhood violence, even family economic hardships (Bethel et al. 2014). Children's ability to weather (navigate) through the many obstacles that they will face requires them to find strength in vulnerability, and to work through those obstacles in spite of the potential outcomes. I strongly believe this is "weathering and recovering," at its best.

Building and fostering resilience in children, in times of adversity, is necessary more than ever because of the times we're living in today. It doesn't matter a child's race, color or creed; their socioeconomic position, neighborhood background, or family origin, resilience is necessary.

Identifying and understanding resilience is critical for every child. I'm a realist so I realize resilience won't stop problems from arising, neither magically cause them to disappear however, having resilience will help children see beyond their problems, and find answers to enjoy life without being overcome with stress.

Key Considerations Concerning Resilience

Resilience is born out of, forged through, and developed through adversity.

When a child experiences adversity his or her strength to overcome becomes a building block of DNA. The ability for children to adapt, persevere, and grow increases exponentially as they face and deal with adversity. It's in moments of trouble, hardship, and crisis that a child must determine to adjust and push forward regardless of the hurt, pain, and suffering. When a child learns to look adversity in the face and be resolute to continue pushing forward is when resilience shines so bright.

Resilience is a process that develops with time

How children deal with trauma, stress, and adversity takes time. We may not see the effects of what has happened to children but as they matriculate though life, from birthday to birthday, from grade to grade, and through various relationships we will have a better idea as to the impact the aforementioned events will have on their lives.

Experiencing distress does not diminish a child's resilience

Although depression, anxiety, and stress may be symptomatic of adverse experiences, it should not lead onlookers to believe a child is not resilient. Children can be dealing with everyday challenges such as family issues, challenges in school, and peer problems all while still being resilient.

Overcoming challenges through resilience often lead to personal growth

A high school student once told me that working through setbacks in life helped create a sense of urgency to keep pushing ahead, and pursuing a path that would lead to college. This student, as result of adversity, gained an increased sense of meaning as they dealt with, and continued forward in spite of the adversity experienced. We must never underestimate how setbacks, challenges, and trials can help students grasp a more significant motivation to work through, around, even during tumultuous times.

The way resilience manifest can change at different stages of life

Dr. Bhatnager says, "One way of thinking or acting might be more helpful at one point in someone's life, but not at another. Think about a child who has no one to turn to in their life – they need to be self-sufficient and scrappy to survive and thrive. But when they get older and have more people around them who care for them, reaching out and asking for help in tough times would be a marker of personal resilience." (Bhatnager, 2002)

Resilience is shaped by the environment and circumstances

The focus here means that resilience is not just an internal trait but is influenced by a person's environment, relationships, culture, and circumstances. The ability to adapt and recover from challenges depends on factors such as support systems, access to resources, and past experiences.

A student's resilience in school may depend on supportive teachers, a safe learning environment, and personal coping strategies. Similarly, a student facing trauma may demonstrate resilience differently based on their social connections and community resources.

Why my pursuit with identifying and understanding resilience?

While attending and presenting at a conference (Innovative Schools Summit) in Orlando, Florida I heard a question asked of a presenter concerning trauma. The question was asked how does resilience play a role in children working through trauma. This question not only captured my attention but has fueled me to pursue the essence of resilience as it relates to its impact on children in school facing adverse situations, circumstances, even conditions. I further sought to correlate how building resilience in schools is critical in this day and time.

Resilience is adapting and recovering in the face of challenges. Children won't and can't avoid hardships therefore, it is crucial for them to learn to develop the capacity to navigate difficulties with perseverance and hope. For children in school, resilience plays a critical role in their emotional well-being, academic success, and social development.

Resilience is key in many areas academically for example:

<u>Emotional regulation</u> – resilient students learn to manage difficulty, disappointment, and overcome fear and doubt.

<u>Academic performance</u> - resilient students are better prepared to work through test anxiety, curriculum changes, and unexpected changes.

<u>Social relationships</u> - resilient students have better relationships with peers, and can work towards solving conflicts with peers, and seek adult support when needed.

<u>Behavioral adaptability</u> - resilient students use coping skills to overcome problems related to home, deal with transitions, and manage expectations without being overwhelmed.

<u>Sustained achievement</u> – resilient children, via weathering and recovering from adversity, are equipped with skills that allow them to navigate challenging experiences, learn from setbacks, and drive through adverse situations, which ultimately lead to sustained academic success.

Also, educational practitioners have long played and continue to play a pivotal role in fostering resilience by creating supportive environments in their classrooms, implementing and practically applying restorative practices, and teaching applicable coping skills. Trauma-informed approaches, strong teacher-student relationships, and access to mental health resources can all contribute to a school and climate that nurtures resilience.

As I move to conclude this chapter let me share that Resilience in education is not developed on calm days when every student is engaged, every lesson flows perfectly, and every parent's email ends

FACING AND OVERCOMING ADVERSITY

with gratitude. It is forged in the unpredictable moments when technology fails, when a student shuts down emotionally, and when behavior erupts unexpectedly, or when your lesson plan doesn't' flow as planned. Resilience manifests when your heart is tired, the data feels discouraging, and yet you still show up and your mind is ready, heart open, determined to try again.

Educators don't just teach resilience; they live it. They model it every time they adapt, rethink, support, or start over. Resilience in the classroom is not about perfection, it's about persistence. It's not about having all the answers, it's about believing there is still a solution worth finding.

Resilience is the quiet strength behind every teaching practitioner who says, "Today was hard. Tomorrow, I'll try again; better, wiser, stronger." It is the fuel of hope, the anchor of purpose, and the heartbeat of every classroom where growth is more important than perfection.

Chapter 2 – Why the Science of Resilience Matters

The science of resilience explores how people, especially children and adults in demanding contexts, adapt, recover, and grow despite stress, adversity, and trauma. Its importance lies in several key areas that we will address.

Instead of defining individuals by problems or risk factors, resilience research helps us see the protective factors such as supportive relationships, coping skills, hope, purpose, and environments that heal rather than harm.

The science of resilience shows that the brain is elastic, skills like emotional regulation, problem-solving, and stress management can be developed. This means resilience isn't a personality trait but teachable and buildable.

Resilience calls attention to conditions that help people thrive. In other words, resilience is manifested in safe relationships, equitable environments, predictable structure, and communities that cultivate belonging. Schools, health systems, and workplaces can design policies and cultures that buffer stress and promote well-being. Research shows resilience supports mental health, improves academic and life outcomes, reduces risk behaviors, and strengthens emotional and physical well-being across the lifespan.

Resilience science provides a narrative of possibility. It should be noted that adversity does not define destiny. When the right supports and skills are in place, people can recover, grow, and often become stronger and more compassionate because of what they've overcome.

I am convinced that resilience science equips teachers to respond with compassion, trauma-awareness, restorative practices, and strategies that build competence, connection, and confidence.

Practical Application of Resilience Science in K–12 Education: An Evidence-Based Perspective

Resilience in children and adolescents is not merely an individual trait; it is a dynamic, interactional process shaped by biology, relationships, environment, and opportunities for growth (Masten, 2014). The science of resilience demonstrates that the brain is highly responsive to context. Supportive environments, strong relationships, predictable structures, and intentional skill-building can significantly strengthen a student's capacity to adapt and thrive despite adversity (National Scientific Council on the Developing Child, 2015).

Understanding these scientific foundations allows educators to intentionally create classroom environments and school systems that buffer stress, support regulation, and promote optimal learning and development.

Resilience Depends on Safety and Regulation

The ability to learn, think clearly, and behave appropriately is deeply connected to the functioning of the stress-response system. When students experience prolonged or intense stress without adequate support, the body shifts into a state of survival, reducing capacity for attention, memory, reasoning, and behavioral control (Perry & Szalavitz, 2006).

Implication for Classrooms

Emotionally safe and predictable environments reduce hyperarousal and allow higher-order thinking to occur. Classroom practices such as calm adult responses, consistent structure, relational tone, and non-shaming discipline contribute to regulation and improved learning outcomes (Bath, 2008; Brunzell, Stokes, & Waters, 2016).

Relationships Are the Primary Protective Factor

A consistent research finding is that the strongest predictor of resilience in youth is the presence of at least one stable, nurturing, and supportive adult relationship (Masten, 2001). Relationships buffer stress, promote neural regulation, and communicate worth and belonging (National Scientific Council on the Developing Child, 2015).

Implication for Schools

Intentional relationship-building practices such as personal check-ins, positive teacher-student interactions, mentoring structures, and restorative approaches—enhance resilience while also reducing behavioral incidents and improving engagement (Furlong, O'Brennan, & You, 2011).

Resilience Requires Explicit Skill-Building

Resilient students are not simply "naturally strong"; they are equipped with emotional, cognitive, and social skills developed over time. These include emotional awareness, self-regulation, problem-solving, communication, perseverance, and adaptive thinking (Compas et al., 2017).

Implication for Instruction

Schools enhance resilience when they integrate:

- Social-emotional learning instruction
- Emotional literacy development

- Explicit regulation strategies (breathing, grounding, reflection)
- Opportunities for students to practice coping and problem-solving

Evidence supports that SEL programming leads to improved academic outcomes, reduced behavioral concerns, and better long-term well-being (Durlak et al., 2011).

Meaning, Purpose, and Agency Strengthen Resilience

Students are more likely to persist through difficulty when they perceive their lives and learning as meaningful. Purpose fosters psychological endurance and strengthens motivation (Snyder, 2002). Agency is the belief that one's actions can influence outcomes—and directly supports resilience (Zimmerman, 2002; Ungar, 2015).

Implication for Educators

Classrooms that provide:

- Choice
- Leadership opportunities
- Voice in decision-making

Opportunities to see personal competence and progress create environments that cultivate ownership, dignity, and resilience (Bandura, 1997).

Normalize Struggle as Part of Learning

Research on growth mindset demonstrates that when students view intelligence and ability as malleable rather than fixed, they approach challenges with greater persistence and emotional resilience (Dweck, 2006, p. 215). Likewise, academic resilience is built when struggle is framed as a normal, expected, and valuable part of learning rather than as failure.

Implication for Classrooms

Feedback that emphasizes effort, strategy, and progress rather than innate ability promotes resilience and long-term achievement (Hattie & Timperley, 2007).

Predictability and Structure Reduce Anxiety

Predictable routines and consistent expectations reduce uncertainty, which in turn lowers stress responses and supports cognitive functioning (Shonkoff et al., 2012). Structure does not restrict growth; it creates the safety needed for growth to occur.

Implication for School Practice

Reliable daily schedules, consistent expectations, clear communication, and emotionally stable environments contribute directly to stronger behavior regulation and improved readiness to learn (Bath, 2008).

Adult Resilience Matters

The regulation capacity of adults significantly affects student outcomes. Dysregulated adults unintentionally escalate student dysregulation, while calm, emotionally regulated educators support neural regulation in children (Perry & Szalavitz, 2017). Teacher well-being is therefore both an ethical responsibility and an instructional strategy.

Implication for Schools

Systems that support educator mental health, collegial support, reflective practice, and emotional sustainability produce stronger student resilience and healthier learning environments (Jennings & Greenberg, 2009).

In conclusion, when science and resilience are joined, we move beyond inspirational language and enter a space of intentional, evidence-informed practice. Science helps us understand how resilient systems are built, why certain students thrive despite adversity, and what conditions best nurture strength, healing, and hope. Neuroscience reminds us that the brain is adaptable; it can learn, heal, and rewire through experience, supportive relationships, and consistent emotional safety. Psychology and resilience research demonstrate that skills like self-regulation, meaning-making, cognitive flexibility, and connection are not accidental traits—they can be taught, strengthened, and sustained. Educational science shows that classrooms grounded in belonging, relevance, high expectations, and relational trust create learning environments where resilience naturally grows.

When science informs resilience, we do not simply wish students to be strong—we intentionally cultivate it. We design schools where emotional well-being is not separate from academic success, but a necessary foundation for it. We empower teachers with strategies grounded in research rather than exhaustion. And we build educational communities where resilience becomes a predictable outcome, not a fortunate accident. Science gives resilience credibility, structure, and direction; resilience gives science heart, humanity, and purpose. Joined together, they create the conditions where both teachers and students can thrive, even in the face of adversity.

Chapter 3 – The Nature and Nurture of Resilience

Resilience is one of my favorite things to write about because it represents not only one of my core values but also one of my greatest strengths. It's also the defining characteristic of the work I have the privilege of doing in public education.

I'm convinced that I've always been a resilient person, mostly because, my upbringing demanded me to be so. When things fell apart, I didn't have the luxury of time to wallow, wait or throw a pity-party. When plans failed, I looked to other plans and kept moving forward. In other words, I was resourceful. I wondered if I was predisposed to "weathering and recovering from adversity?" I believe my ability to be resilient came from my wonderful and resilient mother. I learned so much from watching her, and other mentors turn adversity into action with determination.

The debate over whether resilience is based on nature or nurture has been ongoing for decades. Both sides make compelling arguments, suggesting that resilience isn't one or the other but a dynamic interplay between genetic makeup and environmental influence. From a nature perspective, some people appear naturally more resilient due to genetic factors. From a nurture perspective, resilience is shaped by experiences, relationships, and environments.

Supportive relationships, positive role models, and exposure to manageable challenges help build strong coping skills. Secure attachment in early childhood, encouragement, meaningful responsibilities, and even cultural values all contribute to strengthening resilience over time. Schools, communities, and life experiences play a powerful role in cultivating it. So, can anyone become resilient? Research increasingly supports the answer of yes

While genetics may set the stage, resilience is not a fixed trait but a capacity that can be developed, strengthened, and trained. Skills such as emotional regulation, mindfulness, hopefulness, problem-solving, and stress management can all enhance resilience. Building strong social connections, maintaining a growth mindset, practicing gratitude, and learning from setbacks also help individuals recover and thrive.

Understanding resilience as a blend of nature and nurture allows us to move beyond the question of whether we are resilient to the more pertinent question of how we can become more resilient. While some may have a natural predisposition, anyone regardless of background, history, or genetics—can build, strengthen, and sustain resilience through intentional practice, supportive relationships, and environments that nurture growth.

In chapter 1 we shared that resilience was, "weathering and recovering from adversity." It simply means adapting and thriving. This has fascinated psychologists, educators, and researchers for many years. The question is asked why do some individuals recover quickly from hardships while others struggle? This question has fueled the age-old nature versus nurture debate, which seeks to determine whether resilience is primarily a product of genetic inheritance or shaped by life experiences. Many argue that resilience is hardwired into our DNA but again there is no such thing as a resilience gene. Others emphasize the critical role of supportive environments, early childhood experiences, and learned coping mechanisms. I purport the proposition that nature and nurture work together to shape human adaptability and strength.

Resilience in children is not an accident. It is neither fully inherited nor entirely taught but is shaped by both nature and nurture, working together like two hands that mold and strengthen a child's capacity to adapt, cope, and grow through challenges. When talking about whether resilience is nurture vs nature many factors play a significant role. The role of genetics (nature) is unquestionably important. There are biological factors. Such as efficient stress response systems, neural circuitry, immune responses, and epigenetic changes, all influenced by genetics and environmental factors. There are neurological factors such as the ability of the brain to adapt and recover from trauma, stress, and adversity. Also, neural circuits, brain structure, and stress hormones play a significant role.

Let's look at nature as the inner wiring of resilience. Some children seem naturally more adaptable, optimistic, or emotionally steady. These traits are not just personality as they are influenced by genetics, temperament, and brain development. From birth, children possess differing levels of temperament, emotional regulation, and stress control.

First, consider temperament. Some students are naturally more easygoing or flexible, while others are sensitive, intense, or cautious. A student in your classroom may be one who nothing seems to incite a rash emotional response about anything. Another student in your classroom is enraged by the slightest joke, insult, or negative gesture from a peer. Be mindful that a child's temperament can affect how they handle frustration, change, and conflict.

Second, consider emotional regulation capacity. The brain's prefrontal cortex (responsible for decision-making, impulse control, and emotional balance) develops at different rates in children. Therefore, some students may be more naturally equipped to pause, reflect, and calm themselves before reacting. For example: Dennis, a

FACING AND OVERCOMING ADVERSITY

fifth grader, is being laughed at because his peers saw his mother kiss him at drop-off. Dennis chuckles and says, "You guys are so immature." Dennis is able to pause, reflect, and stay calm as he delineates his classmate's behavior towards him.

<u>Third</u>, consider the <u>stress response system</u>. Students have different biological responses to stress. Some recover quickly from setbacks, while others feel overwhelmed for longer periods of time. This is linked to genetics, brain chemistry, and early experiences. Nature gives each student a unique starting point, but it does not determine their finish line. This is where nurture plays a critical role.

Then there's the role of environment or (nurture). The way a student develops helps define how resilient they will become. How secure is the student's attachments? We must consider how supportive the parents are as well as how the child engages in school, relationships, and extra-curricular activities. Is there reinforcement that is positive on part of teachers, community leaders, even family?

I believe both nature and nurture are important. Genetics play a role in the beginning stages of shaping how a child will handle adversity. The environment plays a role in how resilience continues to develop over the life span. I strongly support genetics (nature) however, environment (nurture) a child's life experiences, social support, and learned coping skills play a more significant role in shaping the child's ability to weather and recover from the trials of life.

Think of nature as a student who is anxious, then nurture as a teacher providing predictable routines for the student. Think of nature as an impulsive student, then nurture as a teacher who provides clear boundaries for the student. Think of nature as an introverted student, then nurture as a teacher who uses reflective activities and encouragement for the student. Finally, think of nature as an easily discouraged student, then nurture as a teacher who uses resilient language.

Resilience is not built when barriers are removed. It is a process where students are supported enough to try, allowed to fail, and encouraged to persist. Students need scaffolded challenges. In other words, challenges, tasks, problems difficult enough to cause them to stretch but supported enough to help them through the process.

This discourse on whether resilience is rooted in nature or nurture reveals that it is best understood through a biopsychosocial lens. Genetic predispositions may shape an individual's baseline capacity for stress regulation and emotional adaptability, yet environmental contexts, including secure relationships, cultural influences, and lived experiences, play a critical role in the development and strengthening of resilient behaviors. Rather than a static trait, resilience emerges as a dynamic, malleable process influenced by both inherited factors and intentional cultivation. This understanding underscores the importance of designing supportive environments, policies, and interventions that promote resilience across diverse populations, irrespective of individual starting points.

To end this chapter, I would like to share a familiar story about "Two Seeds." Two seeds were planted on the same day, but in very different places. The first seed fell on rich soil beside a quiet river. It was surrounded by warmth, steady sunlight, and gentle rain. Its roots grew easily, pushing into soft earth, drawing nourishment without struggle. Everything around it supported its growth. This seed represented nurture—a supportive environment that builds resilience through stability, encouragement, and protection.

The second seed landed in rocky ground on the side of a windy hill. The soil was thin, water was scarce, and every day it faced the force of harsh winds. Its roots had to fight for depth, anchoring around stones and cracks. It grew slowly, bending and stretching toward whatever light it could find. Day after day it endured what other seeds never had to face. This seed represented nature—the innate drive to survive, adapt, and push forward even when resources are limited.

As the years passed, both seeds became trees—but they were not the same. The tree by the river grew tall and straight, supported by the steady environment that nurtured it. The tree on the hill grew shorter and more rugged, its trunk thicker, its roots deeper than anyone imagined. It had weathered storms the other tree never knew. Though shaped by hardship, it had developed a strength and stability uniquely its own.

Both trees were resilient—but their resilience came from different sources. The river tree's resilience was built through nurture—consistent support, a safe environment, and the steady presence of what it needed. The hill tree's resilience was shaped by nature—innate grit, adaptation, and the ability to grow through pressure.

Together, their story shows a powerful truth - Resilience is not formed in only one way. Some students develop it because they were nurtured well. Others develop it because life forced them to. And many grow resilient through a blend of both - innate strength supported by caring adults who help them flourish.

Chapter 4 – Why Is Resilience Important

The importance of resilience in school-aged children, from my perspective, should not be overestimated. In times of despair, desperation, and doubt resilience can be the x-factor that propels a student to stay in school in spite the road that appears long and winding. When life for a child in school appears to be overwhelming and dark the resilient student can pull from their reservoir of resilience strategies to look beyond past failure, hardships, and problems their facing, ultimately looking to the future for hope that transcends adversity.

Isn't it amazing how our students can be naturally resilient? I'm always amazed watching a student's bounce back from adversity. Challenges, disappointments, and failure comes with the territory for k-12 students. It's refreshing to see students struggle academically but overcome. It's even better when students forging ahead to the next challenge to conquer, the next obstacle to negotiate, and the next lesson to learn how to weather and overcome adversity. That being said, parents, educators, mental health workers everywhere should come to embrace that resilience is an ability that children can develop and that can and will be influenced by various environmental factors. It's fact that resilience isn't a fixed trait that you simply have or don't have but a dynamic ability to conquer barriers that's supported by other protective factors and essential relational skills.

The American Psychological Association defines resilience as "the process and outcome of successfully adapting to difficult or challenging life experiences, especially through mental, emotional, and behavioral flexibility and adjustment to external and internal demands."

So, why is resilience necessary for students of all ages? When we consider research, much analysis has associated resilience to various outcomes, such as, academic success, higher connections, better stress management, and increased well-being. Students who exhibit resilience were determined to report greater levels of school involvement, and task focused.

When we consider the context of social skills enhancement, resilience is distinct because it isn't an independent ability or result like emotion management, self-awareness, relationship-building, or problem-solving. While similar, it's more exact to think of resilience as a potential constructed on the foundation of the aforementioned proficiencies. Resilience, though many definitions have been communicated, and it has various components, doesn't mean it isn't necessary. Many educators have come to recognize resilience as an important ability that a student should develop.

What skills can help students build the skills they need to be resilient? What follows are a number of ways social emotional learning programs can help students build the skills that manifest resilience. These skills aid students in navigating the intricacies of life in and out of school.

Resilience requires emotion management. Resilience is not stifling a student's emotions in the face of adversity. Instead, resilience arises from a student's ability to understand and manage the difficult emotions that originate in the face of adversity such as fear, frustration, anger, even sadness.

A core personal competency is Self-management, which encompasses a student's ability to manage their emotions, as well as an ingredient in building resilience. Like adults, kids experience myriads of emotions all the time, but especially when dealing with adversity.

Social emotional learning enables students to identify and manage emotions. It gives students strategies to name and understand how their emotions help them work through adversity. This knowledge and these strategies could make the difference between a student either becoming stressed and quitting when difficulties arise, and continuing to deal with the adversity and move forward.

Interpersonal skills support resilience. Resilience is an individual skill however, it is also, as much as we may think of resilience as an individualized skill, resilience is also developed on a student's ability to form and maintain healthy, supportive relationships. You have heard the saying, "When the going gets tough, the tough get going." Contrary to this adage, students who are resilient look for and rely on others for support.

The ability to build and maintain healthy relationships is a foundational personal and relational competency as well as a central focus of many classroom-based human skills programs and interventions. These programs provide students with meaningful opportunities to observe, understand, and practice healthy relationship skills in real classroom settings. This can include a wide range of skills, from managing conflict to interacting effectively with people who are different from themselves.

As children develop their ability to connect with and depend on others, they become better equipped to navigate challenging experiences. When obstacles arise, children with strong relationship skills understand that they don't have to face them alone—they have friends, family, and teachers who can support them when they fail an algebra test, don't make the soccer team, or lose someone they love.

FACING AND OVERCOMING ADVERSITY

These healthy relationship skills help them process, cope with, and work through life's difficult moments.

Responsible decision-making raises resilience. Another key to understanding resilience in children is recognizing the role of decision-making. Responsible decision-making is a core competency that includes curiosity, open-mindedness, the ability to make reasoned judgments after analyzing information, identifying solutions to personal and social problems, and anticipating the consequences of one's actions. These skills directly support a child's capacity to navigate and overcome challenges.

I will now tell you a story that will help you identify how resilience helps students, through responsible decision-making. Let me take you back in time to John Adams High School in Cleveland, Ohio. The year was 1978. I was a freshman (10th grade). I had come to the school as a touted Junior High Track & Field athlete looking to bolster the already loaded team of, and long history of phenomenal sprinters. The man I still refer to as my surrogate father, James Patterson, was coach and responsible for my development. I was coming off a good indoor season, and was poised to help the team win a State Championship. I had worked my way into being one of the top sprinters on the team, and member of the potential State Champion 4 x200 relay.

It was the custom that if another teammate wanted to challenge another relay member for a spot on the relay, he could do so by requesting what coach called a "Runoff." I was challenged of all people. I didn't believe I should have been challenged being one of the top sprinters on the team however, life came at me face that day in the Spring of 1978. Four young men (students) lined up at the 200-meter start line. The gun went off and away we went. The outcome was I finished 3rd, meaning I would not be on the 4 x 200 relay for the upcoming meet as only the top 2 joined the relay.

Defeated, deflated, and disgusted, I picked up my sweats and vacated the track saying, "I quit." I went to the locker room to gather my belongings only to encounter coach Patterson who walked in saying, "Marty, disappointments will happen, things will not always go your way." He then said something that even as I write, brings tears to my eyes, but forever changed my life. Coach said, "Marty, you have a choice. Put your sweats and shoes back on and get to the track or allow defeat to define who you are." Needless to say, I made my way back to the track and the rest is history. Moving forward, I experienced many defeats but resilience had been forged and I was better as result of the defeat that day.

Defeat and Coach Patterson's words caused me to make a decision to continue becoming resilient. I was able to "weather and recover from adversity." Responsible decision-making raised my ability to be resilient. Further, I believe every student should have the blessing of a Principal, Teacher, Coach to help them learn to "weather and recover from adversity."

Resilience, then, isn't about rigid strength or simply "pushing through" adversity. Another helpful illustration is surfing—sometimes catching the wave, sometimes missing it, and continually adjusting to the motion of the ocean around you. Similarly, children who have developed resilience are able to respond to difficulties with flexibility, think critically about their situation, and make thoughtful decisions about how to move forward.

The benefits of resilience in children are almost too many to name. Resilience helps them stay connected with others, remain motivated in school and extracurricular activities, and build confidence. It fuels academic success, supports emotional well-being, and lays the groundwork for long-term personal and social growth.

While there's no single formula for building resilience in students, comprehensive human skills instruction in the classroom is a powerful foundation. Core competencies—such as relationship skills, emotional regulation, and responsible decision-making—equip children with the tools needed to adapt, persevere, and thrive. These strengths shape not just their school experience, but their development for years to come.

The question of resilience being important is easy for me to answer and should bring clarity as to why every student should learn, develop, and grow from adversity. When answering this question, I considered my own life as a student growing up in the inner-city of Cleveland, Ohio. The adversity experienced was palpable. My parents divorced and after the divorce, at the age of 11, I experienced growing up in a single parent home for most of my early school life. I realized quickly that divorce meant instability in the home as my mother struggled to raise four children. Adversity would come in many shapes, sizes and forms. There were times of food insecurity, utilities not paid (some of you know what that looks and feels like), and the inability of my mother to not have the finances for me to participate in extra-curricular sporting activities.

It was in the aforementioned times, that resilience continued to form. Learning how to weather and recover from adversity would become a common theme as I negotiated life minute by minute, hour by hour, day by day, week by week, month by month, and year by year. I would learn that when one door closed, I was to look for another door. A great example was at age ten, I had a best friend named Henry who live 6 houses from me. His father would ask if I could go to Niagara Falls with them. My parents said yes however, on the day of the trip my mother was unable to provide monies necessary for me to take the trip. It was in this time of disappointment that I began working a paper route to earn money so that I could engage in certain desired activities.

Life would again teach me resilience at a young age when in Junior High I thought being involved and good in sports meant I could be a slouch in the classroom. My track coach, during my 7th grade year, informed me that unless I could maintain a 2.5% grade average, I wouldn't be allowed to run track. The conversation came at the time I was carrying a 1.9% grade average. I informed my mother of the conversation with my coach and she confirmed my greatest fear. My mother, though she didn't graduate from high school, was a staunch advocate of education ultimately said, "You will not run until you arrive at your intended grade point average of 2/5%.

It was in those six weeks prior to the start of the track season that I would learn resilience. I struggled in science and math. I stayed after school with my teachers, used tutors, and worked tirelessly to achieve the goal of the required 2.5% grade average. I learned the power of resilience in those days when my friends were practicing, playing, and enjoying life.

The last example I want to share with you, as to why resilience is important, takes place in college. It was my freshman year at Kent State University. I was in college on a track & field scholarship. Because of my low-grade point average out of high school (yes, I being an extraordinary athlete caused me to again believe I didn't need to focus in class), I was put in remedial English. My instructor (I can't remember her name) was tough on me. I would turn in papers and she would return them with red ink, meaning the papers were below standard. I would often leave class frustrated, angry, even bewildered as to why my papers were sub-standard.

I decided to ask for a meeting with her. After class I had the courage (resilience) to ask for help. That day changed my life as she shared with me how to write better, learning good writing mechanics. The end of the semester would come and though I would only earn a "C" in her class it taught me the power of resilience as I would spend hours using the mechanics, strategies, and tools she provided so that I could learn to write. I'm forever indebted to my instructor for then I didn't realize I would need the skills she provided for me to become the writer I've become today.

Chapter 5 – The Foundations of Resilience

The foundation of resilience is built on key elements that allow children to adapt, recover, and grow through challenges. In this chapter I will address four main pillars that allow resilience to manifest in the lives of students.

The first pillar is **Self-awareness**: This pillar helps children respond thoughtfully rather than impulsively. Self-awareness is critical for personal growth and well-being. Self-awareness focuses on helping children understand their emotions, triggers, strengths, and limits. There are many skills we could elaborate on however, increasing self-awareness is an essential cornerstone to building emotional intelligence and resilience.

When we encourage young pliable minds to be mindful of their thoughts and self-talk is used in moments of adversity, we set the foundation for resilience. As parents, educators, and mental health practitioners, we must always dive into the power of challenging negativity, embracing positivity, and understanding emotional landscapes. We are commissioned to teach, planting seeds of self-awareness that will grow into self-discovery and emotional strength.

Increasing self-awareness is pivotal to build resilience in children. Self-awareness allows children to gain insight into their thoughts, emotions, and reactions. Being conscious of their thinking processes and self-talk in the moment helps them develop an understanding of how their minds work.

FACING AND OVERCOMING ADVERSITY

For example, think about a young boy who gets angry during a game because of losing. The child blames everyone accept him or herself. The child is unable to recognize the frustration and instead abruptly decides to disengage from the game. This interplay between recognizing and managing emotions is essential for navigating relationships, handling challenges, setting and achieving goals.

Self-awareness is a necessary component of helping students understand who they are (strengths, needs, and emotions), how they feel (emotional identification), why they feel the way they do (connection between feelings, thoughts, and behavior), and how their actions affect others (social impact and perspective-taking).

Self-awareness can manifest in various situations and circumstances. Recognition plays a role as a student may say, "I'm feeling frustrated with a math problem; I need to take a break." The student might say, "This is hard, but I will ask for help." Self-awareness is the student understanding their learning style, stress patterns, or motivators. Self-awareness is the building block for other social emotional learning skills because students can't regulate what they cannot recognize.

Resilience, with self-awareness as a foundational block, has many looks. It may look like a student trying again after receiving a low grade. It could look like a student recovering from conflict with a classmate. It could look like a student trying to navigate change at home or school with a trusted teacher, coach, even administrator. It could look like a student believing their efforts can create a better future.

Let's ask a question. How does self-awareness build resilience? When students can identify emotions, triggers, and strengths, they are more equipped to:

- Make application of coping strategies that work for them

- Hesitate before reacting impulsively
- Promote their own needs
- Contemplate on difficulties without self-disgust
- Repair their confidence after setbacks

Research abounds with information on how when students are enveloped in trauma-informed environments, self-awareness becomes a protective factor, giving them a sense of agency when life feels uncertain. Goleman (1995) explains that resilient individuals are able to advocate for themselves, engage in effective problem solving, and to seek support when they need it most.

Why These Skills Matter in Schools

Students with strong self-awareness and resilience are more likely to:

- Engage in learning even when lessons are difficult
- Resolve struggles without escalation
- Form positive relationships with peers and adults
- Endure through academic adversity
- Regulate emotions in healthy ways instead of through dysregulated behavior

The second pillar is **connection and support**: Connection is characteristic of good relationships with family, friends, and teachers. Support from an emotional and instructional standpoint aids students with development of skills to navigate adversity. Resilience can be seen when children are involved in community, cultural, and school engagement. Connection and support based upon authentic relationships with trusted people provide encouragement, perspective, and belonging during times of adversity. In fact, connection is one of Alison Block's 5 protective factors that promote resilience (Block, 2021).

FACING AND OVERCOMING ADVERSITY

Connection matters and is a strong predictor of resilience in children. Connection acts as a buffer against stress, trauma, and academic pressure. When students feel connected and supported, they experience:

- Increased emotional safety
- Better self – regulation
- Higher engagement and attendance
- Stronger identity and sense of belonging
- Reduced behavioral challenges

Support comes in many forms that build resilience. There's emotional support, academic and instructional support, and social support. Students provided emotional support receive it by way of warmth, empathy, and active listening. When students have predictable routines and direction provided by school faculty they can trust, great things happen.

Resilience is built when faculty provides clear expectations, scaffolding is used, and skill-building is learned in the classroom. Teachers play a role that cannot be denied, nor demised.

Resilience, lastly, is built on peer connections (peers learning and growing together), collaborative learning (students working together in pairs or groups), and restorative (strengthens relationships, build community, and create environments where students feel valued, heard, and connected) implemented on a consistent basis.

The third pillar is **Purpose and meaning** – Having a sense of "why" fuels perseverance. Purpose turns pain into motivation and struggle into growth. When students understand why their pursuit of education matters, they are more apt to persevere. When the work of fulfilling dreams, and goals challenge students purpose becomes their fuel to keep going even though they feel overwhelmed. Further, purpose strengthens students drive, and increases their willingness to try again after failure occurs.

Purpose gives direction when adversity arises. Resilience motivates a student to recover and reorient after a challenge, failure, defeat. They know what's necessary as they make sense of the setbacks, and are more likely to see failure as feedback rather than final. Purpose builds identify and promotes a sense of self-worth. Students with purpose internalize, then view themselves as competent, capable, and valuable. Students with purpose say things like, "I can handle this," "I'm pressing on towards something much bigger than what's happening right now."

As a kid growing up in inner-city of Cleveland, I found it necessary to have purpose for everything I did. It didn't matter if it was running track, playing football or passionately engaged in a friendly game of electric football with my cousins (Eric Anderson and Darryl Anderson). Not knowing that resilience was the reason behind my purposeful drive, I was one to not give up easily because my "why" was bigger than obstacles before me. Purpose fueled my persistence, especially when whatever I was doing became difficult.

Hope is another ingredient of resilience, in fact, hope anchors resilience. A student with purpose has a reason to believe in the possibility of a promising future even when present circumstances are prevailing. A great example of resilience anchored by hope is meeting a young teenager at Choffin Career & Technical Center in the fall of 2024. She'd been kicked out of her home by her parents. She was living from pillar to post. What caught my attention was that she was happy, socially engaged with peers, focused on attending Ohio State University, although sleeping on her boyfriend's couch. I was looking for anger, anxiety, bitterness and resentment but found resilience anchored by hope. Psychologist Chan Hellman believes hope is measurable and, therefore, predictive of success (Hellman, 2018). Purpose turns challenges into stepping stones, not a derailment. It helps students navigate beyond the moment, believe in their potential, and continue moving forward with strength and clarity.

The fourth pillar is **Adaptability and problem-solving** – This has a focus on how students adjust, stay flexible, and find solutions when life isn't going as planned. This pillar of resilience is then rooted and grounded in a sense of self, strengthened by connection, guided by purpose, and sustained by adaptability.

Students, with help, can realize that everything is not a failure, setback or threat. One doesn't have to be a rocket scientist to know that adaptability is a challenge for many students, especially grades k -12. When students learn and make practical application of being adaptable their ability to be resilient will improve exponentially.

Adaptability is critical for students for many reasons. Let's consider a student moving to another school district. The student will have to adapt to a new bus to ride, new peers to meet, and even a new curriculum to learn in the classroom. Surely this student will leave home feeling anxious about the new school. The student must navigate the thoughts, feelings, and anxiety adjustments, way of thinking, and how to move forward and ultimately adapt.

Adaptability will help students deal with the change that so often happens in their lives. Routines will shift, expectations change, and unexpected challenges occur. When they can adapt it strengthens their resilience. It teaches students that sometimes changes happen, that being flexible is critical, and that change can be handled.

Problem-solving goes hand in hand with adaptability. It gives students the ability to deal with barriers head on. Strategy replaces panic allowing students to build a robust resilience. Students become better equipped to break challenges into manageable steps. Students, when having problem-solving skills, are able to think through options in challenging times and deal with the consequences of their decisions. A student with problem-solving skills learns from their mistakes, allowing resilience to take center stage by not giving up.

In a nutshell we can be clear that adaptability assist students with facing change. On the other hand, problem-solving assist and helps students manage their challenges. When you put both together, they form a solid backbone of resilience.

Chapter 6 – Identifying and Understanding Risk and Protective Factors

Promoting resilience calls for an understanding of the protective and risk factors in a young person's life. Protective factors enhance the probability that a student will be resilient and mollify negative influences. Alternatively, risk factors can form hurdles and impede a student's ability to develop resilience.

Academic institutions play a central part in actuating student's resilience. Students spend countless hours, five days a week, in or around the classroom. As a result, schools can be contributory in providing protective factors and limiting risk factors for their students.

Further, Identifying and understanding risk and protective factors are central to building resilient students. These factors influence how students respond to adversity, manage stress, and develop the internal strength to thrive despite challenges in and out of the classroom.

Resilience is inhibited by risk factors and promoted by protective factors (Alvord & Grados, 2005; Benzies & Mychasiuk, 2009; Fergus & Zimmerman, 2005; Martinez-Torteya, Bogat, von Eye, & Levendosky, 2009; Masten et al., 1991; Rak & Patterson, 1996; Walsh, 2003). Protective factors alter responses to adverse events so that potential negative outcomes can be avoided. On the other hand, risk factors are circumstances that increase the probability of poor outcomes. Protective and risk factors are not stationary units; they change in relation to context leading to different outcomes (Walsh, 2003).

Risk factors are conditions or influences that increase the likelihood of negative outcomes. Risk Factors manifest in various ways to name a few there is trauma, poverty and socioeconomic challenges. There is violence, parental substance abuse, and lack of access to resources. There is negative family dynamics, family, and health issues. There is bullying, limited opportunities for positive experiences, and lack of social-emotional learning.

The aforementioned risk factors play a significant role regardless of where a student lives and/or how they may be parented. Students can have high GPA's even low GPA's and still be enveloped by risk factors. Students, whether m two parent families or broken homes, can still encounter risk factors that can create academic stress, poor coping skills, and academic struggles.

Many factors play a role in risk factors challenging our students in and out of the classroom. In the first-place risk factors can be a detriment. Risk factors can cause students to disengage academically, have poor attendance, which currently plagues our schools across the country. Students with high risk factors, not helped, are prone to drop out. Often times students dealing with risk factors don't have the support at home necessary to work through, and/or overcome academic challenges. Limited resources can impact students especially when they have limited resources such as books, after-school help, and use of technology.

In the second place, there are emotional and mental health effects that cause anxiety, depression, and bullying to name a few (Esch, P., Bocquet, V., Pull, C., et al. (2014). The downward spiral of mental disorders and educational attainment. Social Psychiatry and Psychiatric Epidemiology, 49, 129-139. Often times students have difficulty staying focused and their ability to process information is manifested. Many times, students can engage in "learned helplessness," as they often communicate a lack of belief in their abilities.

In the third place, many at risk students show behavior not conducive to classroom learning. There's aggression, defiance, and many times withdrawal from peers. At risk students have difficulty staying in school (suspensions) even disciplinary actions. Many times, teachers label these students saying, "they are incorrigible, unmotivated, and troubled." There's no doubt that when students can't communicate what they're feeling, behavior is the by product.

In the fourth place, many students are challenged socially. When students grow up in homes that are unstable (single parents, poor environments) they struggle to form good/healthy relationships. Many times, we will see students, whom have not been able to navigate risk factors, feel out of touch with peers, experience rejection, and exclusion. Being socially connected in school forms a protective umbrella, helping students be less vulnerable.

In the fifth place, when students are experiencing risk factors, their ability to hope and be resilient is weakened leading to poor self-actualization, difficulty working through problems, and an inability to forecast their futures. Hope is looking beyond the horizon to see the shore of possibilities. Dreams and goals are empowered by hope and resilience.

Finally, there is a cumulative effect on students when risk factors overwhelm them. I've seen many students in Youngstown City School District show symptoms of stress, emotional overload, even being overwhelmed by challenges they should be able to navigate.

Risk factors don't define a student but they can limit their opportunities unless balanced by protective factors like support, relationships, and resilience building environments.

Protective factors are conditions or influences that buffer against risk, promote resilience, and support positive outcomes. Schools and mental health establishments can help produce students who are healthy and resilient by being calculated, systematic, and complementary in their approach. When teaching/mental health practitioners build protective factors into students' everyday life, risky behaviors such as substance abuse, violence, and school dropout can substantially be diminished.

There is no question about the positive influence protective factors have on building a foundation of resilience in students. Not a day goes by while driving to my office at Choffin Career & Technical Center (Youngstown City School District) that I don't brood over ways to be a positive influence in the lives of the scholars (students are called scholars in our district) within my spacial order or proximity. So, lets peruse the landscape of protective factors that build resilience in children and students alike. I'm mindful that research has indicated many protective factors however, I will account for those that promote resilience in students.

Relationship is a protective factor that seems to make its way to the top of any protective factors list when related to resilience in students. Parents, family and teachers, coaches are the adults who daily play a role in the process of building and promoting resilience. Then there's community, cultural, and faith-based relationships that promote resilience. When students are able to internalize the aforementioned relationships, they find connectedness which promotes resilience.

FACING AND OVERCOMING ADVERSITY

Kirsten Weir says, "Researchers agree that of all the factors that boost resilience, good parenting is often the most significant" (Weir, 2017, p. 40). Phillip Fisher, Ph.D. a professor of psychology at the University of Oregon, says, "The biggest difference, over and above one's genetic blueprint, is the relationship a child has with a primary caregiver." Time and time again I've seen students who are resilient and exhibit resilient tendencies and at the core of their resilience is a parent, or adult figure. I'm a living witness of the quotes by Weir and Fisher that resilience is boosted by good parenting. My mother (Verta Freeman) continuously said to me, "Always give your best at whatever you do," my grandmother (Bertha Anderson) would say, "Remember the little engine that said I think I can," and my high school track coach and consummate educator (James Patterson) who would say, "Natural ability will take you but so far, hard work will take you further." All the previous mentioned individuals played vital roles in promoting my resilience.

Being an example promotes resilience by modeling attitudes, behaviors, and coping strategies you, as a teacher, or any adult for that matter, want students to develop. By promoting resilience students are given a living blueprint for how to navigate adversity. Children learn far more from what teachers demonstrate than from what they declare, and consistent, authentic modeling becomes a powerful source of emotional and behavioral guidance.

When teachers and caregivers model calm problem-solving, flexible thinking, and healthy emotional expression, students begin to internalize those same skills. A student observing a teacher handle stress with composure, acknowledge mistakes without shame, and persevere through challenges shows them that setbacks are not signs of failure but opportunities to grow. This builds confidence and reduces fear of trying, failing, and trying again.

Likewise, when adults model empathy, inclusivity, and respectful communication, students learn how to build strong relationships, which is one of the strongest predictors of resilience. Modeling also creates psychological safety: when students watch teachers/adults own their emotions, repair harm, or ask for help, they realize that vulnerability is not weakness but strength.

Ultimately, being an example gives students a real-life roadmap for resilience. It shows them what resilience looks like in action and empowers them to mirror those behaviors in their own lives, helping them develop the internal tools needed to thrive despite challenges.

Shaping the environment is a protective factor that builds resilience. Although many factors predisposing resilience are intrinsic, developing resilience necessitates a multilayered and unified approach. The school plays a significant role in students learning ecosystem. Schools must provide an environment conducive to a positive environment. Students should be afforded consistent, predictable, and clear expectations and boundaries that allow them to thrive. When the culture and climate of a school is positive, and optimistic it should and will produce resilient students.

I'm thrilled every time I enter Rayen Early College Middle School in Youngstown City School District. This is because the culture and climate of the school exudes consistency, is predictable, and the positive atmosphere lends itself to a learning ecosystem. The principal (Dr. Maureen Donofrio and faculty) begins from day one of the school year creating and maintaining an environment that every student can learn to abide within. The students enjoy the learning process, build positive relationships, and continuously produce grades indicative of an environment that has been shaped for success.

Communication is a vital protective factor that strengthens resilience by nurturing connection, clarity, and coping in students.

FACING AND OVERCOMING ADVERSITY

When young people are encouraged to express their thoughts and emotions openly, they develop a sense of belonging and trust that anchors them during challenging moments.

Clear and compassionate communication from teachers, or any adult, reduces confusion and stress, creating an environment where students feel safe to ask questions, make mistakes, and seek support. As students learn to articulate their needs, navigate conflict, and engage in collaborative problem-solving they build the social and emotional skills that empower them to adapt in times of adversity. Over time, the supportive language they hear becomes the positive inner voice that fuels their confidence, persistence, and hope. In this way, communication does far more than exchange information, it cultivates the conditions in which resilience can truly grow.

Establishing a culture of inclusivity promotes resilience in K–12 students by constructing a climate where every student can experience a sense of being valued, accepted, and supported. This is a key point in helping students deal with adversity. When students experience a sense of belonging, they are more likely to engage, take academic risks, and trust the adults around them.

Inclusivity reduces feelings of isolation, which is one of the greatest barriers to resilience, and instead fosters psychological safety—a foundation that allows students to express emotions, seek help, and try again after setbacks. In inclusive classrooms, diverse perspectives and backgrounds are honored, teaching students empathy, perspective-taking, and collaborative problem-solving skills. These experiences help them navigate social challenges with confidence.

Furthermore, inclusivity ensures that students see themselves reflected in the curriculum, the environment, and the school culture, reinforcing positive identity development and strengthening their internal sense of worth. Ultimately, a culture of inclusivity builds a supportive network around students, equipping them with the emotional, social, and relational resources needed to thrive despite the challenges they face.

Self-control promotes resilience in students because it equips them with the ability to manage their emotions, behaviors, and impulses when faced with challenges. When students develop self-control, they learn to pause before reacting, giving themselves space to choose responses that support problem-solving rather than escalate stress. This ability to regulate emotions helps them stay grounded during difficult moments, reducing the likelihood of feeling overwhelmed or defeated.

Self-control also strengthens resilience by empowering students to persist toward long-term goals even when short-term frustrations arise. Students who can refocus their attention, delay gratification, and resist distractions are better able to stay engaged academically and socially, which builds confidence and a sense of capability.

Additionally, practicing self-control helps students navigate conflicts more peacefully, maintain positive relationships, and recover more quickly from setbacks—core components of resilience. Ultimately, self-control gives students the internal tools to weather adversity with clarity and composure. It allows them to manage stress, make wise choices, and keep moving forward, which forms a strong foundation for resilient thinking and behavior.

Knowing and building rapport with your students does not grow in isolation; it grows in relationship. One of the most powerful ways educators can strengthen resilience in K–12 students is by intentionally getting to know who their students are, not just academically, but socially, emotionally, and culturally. When teachers understand the whole child, they create learning spaces where students feel seen, valued, and supported. That sense of connection becomes a protective factor that equips students to navigate adversity with confidence.

When students feel known, they experience psychological safety, and the emotional assurance that school is a place where they can take risks, make mistakes, and recover without fear of judgment. This safety opens the door for persistence. A child who trusts their teacher is more willing to try again after failure, more open to feedback, and more capable of regulating emotions in moments of challenge.

Resilience comes by knowing and building rapport with students also builds a deep sense of belonging, which research identifies as one of the strongest predictors of resilience. Belonging communicates, "You matter here." For students carrying trauma, facing instability at home, or struggling socially, a building and classroom environment where they are understood becomes a stabilizing force. Connection is the antidote to isolation, and students who feel connected are more likely to rebound during stressful seasons. I love what Dr. Brene Brown says about connectedness, "I define connection as the energy that exists between people when they feel seen, heard, and valued, when they can give and receive without judgment; and when they derive sustenance and strength from the relationship."

Understanding students' backgrounds, communication styles, and triggers equips educators to respond rather than react. When a teacher knows the story behind a behavior, they shift from punishment to support. Instead of escalating conflict, they guide students through emotional regulation, reflection, and repair skills that resides at the heart of resilience. Knowing and building rapport helps students learn that challenges do not define them; instead, each challenge becomes an opportunity to build stronger coping strategies.

Additionally, knowing students enables teachers to tailor instruction to their strengths and interests, making learning more engaging and meaningful. Personalized motivation fuels persistence. When students see themselves reflected in the curriculum, or when assignments connect to their passions, they are more likely to stay committed through academic struggles.

When an educator honors students' culture, identity, and lived experiences, they strengthen each child's internal sense of worth. A strong identity functions like armor during adversity. Students who know they are valued and who see that their teacher respects who they are should approach challenges with greater confidence, optimism, and hope.

Finally, knowing your students is not a soft skill; it is a resilience strategy. It transforms the classroom from a place of compliance into a community of belonging. It moves teachers from managing behavior to nurturing growth. It ensures that every student, regardless of background, has at least one caring adult investing in their success. When students feel known, they feel safe. When they feel safe, they can learn, take risks, and rise.

Chapter 7 – Adversity as a Teacher: Understanding How Adversity Shapes Resilience

Adversity is often viewed as something to avoid, minimize, or escape. In the lives of students, adversity can show up as academic setbacks, social challenges, family instability, trauma, poverty, or moments of disappointment that press against a child's sense of safety and confidence. While adversity can create barriers to learning, it also carries another truth: adversity can teach, develop, and strengthen the internal skills that form the foundation of resilience. When educators understand adversity, not as a punishment but as a process, they can help students transform difficult experiences into opportunities for growth.

Resilience is not built in comfortable, predictable seasons. It is shaped in moments when students face something they are not sure they can handle. When students receive support, guidance, and encouragement along the way they can overcome adversity and develop resilience that will help them throughout the lifespan. When a child navigates adversity with a caring adult by their side, their brain develops new pathways for problem-solving, emotional regulation, and hope. They begin to learn, "I can do hard things. I can survive difficult moments. I can rise again."

Adversity Builds Inner Strength

Adversity challenges students to stretch beyond their comfort zones. When students encounter frustration in academics, conflicts with peers, or changes in their environment, they learn to manage stress in real time. These experiences strengthen persistence, patience, and adaptability. Each moment of struggle becomes a rehearsal for future challenges. Instead of breaking students, adversity, when supported helps build the emotional muscles that make them stronger.

Adversity Teaches Problem-Solving

When students face obstacles, their brains must shift from reaction to reflection. They begin asking: What are my options? Who can help me? How can I approach this differently?

These questions strengthen executive functioning skills essential for lifelong resilience. Students learn to pause, think, evaluate choices, and make decisions. These skills will serve them not only in school but in relationships, careers, and adulthood.

Adversity Develops Emotional Regulation

Hard moments trigger strong emotions, from frustration to fear. But with the support of a trusted adult, students learn how to identify, express, and manage those emotions in healthy ways. They discover that emotions are signals, not threats. This emotional regulation becomes one of the most powerful resilience tools a student can acquire. A child who can calm themselves, re-center, and continue forward has a lifelong advantage.

Adversity Reveals Identity and Purpose

Adversity often becomes the mirror that helps students see who they are and what they are capable of. When they overcome a difficult moment—no matter how small—they discover internal qualities such as courage, perseverance, and determination. Adversity shows students that their story is not defined by challenges but by how they rise from them. This deepens identity, cultivates confidence, and builds a sense of purpose.

FACING AND OVERCOMING ADVERSITY

Adversity Builds Empathy and Compassion

Students who have faced adversity often develop a heightened awareness of others' struggles. They become more empathetic, more patient, and more capable of offering support to peers. Adversity softens the heart even as it strengthens the mind. It helps students understand that everyone is carrying something and that kindness can make someone else's burden feel lighter.

Teaches Students the Power of Relationships

Children learn resilience not in isolation but in connection. Adversity teaches them that it is okay to ask for help, lean on others, and trust supportive adults. The presence of even one caring adult during adversity can change a student's entire life trajectory. When educators walk alongside students during hard moments, they reinforce the truth that resilience is not built alone—it's built-in community.

Adversity Helps Students Develop Hope

The greatest lesson adversity teaches is hope. When a student encounters a challenge, works through it, and comes out stronger, they learn that setbacks are temporary. They learn to look beyond the moment they are in. Hope becomes the anchor that keeps them grounded during future storms. When students believe that tomorrow holds possibility, resilience becomes their natural response to difficulty.

The Role of Educators in the Adversity-Resilience Cycle

Educators hold a vital role in how students interpret and respond to adversity. Teachers can't remove every challenge, but they can influence whether adversity becomes a barrier or a bridge. When teachers respond with patience, empathy, structure, and encouragement, they help students transform overwhelming moments into empowering ones. Educators become interpreters—helping students understand that adversity is not the end of the story but the beginning of growth. Students learn resilience when an adult says,

"I see your struggle. I believe in you. I'm here to help you through this."

Conclusion: Adversity Is the Classroom of the Heart

In every school, adversity walks through the doors with the students. But adversity does not have to be the villain in the story. It can become the teacher—the one that develops courage, shapes character, and strengthens resilience. With supportive adults, safe environments, and intentional teaching, adversity becomes a catalyst that empowers students to rise stronger, think deeper, and hope brighter. When educators understand how adversity shapes resilience, they become builders of strength, mentors of perseverance, and guides who help students discover the resilience they did not know they had.

Chapter 8 – Educator Resilience: The Heartbeat of a Thriving School

Teaching has always been more than a profession. It is emotional labor, community work, relational leadership, and mission-driven service woven together. Educators carry the weight of students' academic needs, social–emotional challenges, personal stories, trauma histories, and daily uncertainties. Despite these demands, thousands of teachers continue to show up with courage, compassion, and creativity. What sustains them? Resilience.

Defining educator resilience, in its broader context is, "The capacity to bounce back, to recover strength or spirit quickly and efficiently in the face of adversity, and it is closely linked with vocational commitment, self-efficacy, and the motivation to teach" (Sammons et al., 2007, p. 694). Psychology Today says, "Resilience isn't just about coping. It's about sustaining passion, maintaining purpose, and navigating adversity without losing oneself. And as we face escalating complexities in schools—whether it's post-pandemic mental health surges, digital transformation, or staffing crises—resilience may be our most vital asset" Psychology Today, 2025).

Educator resilience is not about perfection, toughness, or never feeling stressed. It is the ongoing process of adapting, recovering, and growing through the challenges inherent in education. It is the internal capacity and external support that allow educators to continue doing meaningful work without losing themselves in the process. Resilience keeps teachers grounded when circumstances change, hopeful when outcomes seem uncertain, and steady when students need stability most.

The Nature of Resilience in Educators

Resilience can manifest in K-12 educators through behaviors that prioritize emotional steadiness, connection, and adaptability. It is visible in how they show up, how they respond, how they recover, and how they continue to care. When educators demonstrate resilience, they not only sustain themselves, they shape the culture of the school, and strengthen their student's capacity to overcome adversity. Resilience is not a trait someone either has or does not have. It is a dynamic skill set shaped by experiences, relationships, beliefs, and environments. For educators, resilience emerges at the intersection of purpose, competence, connection, and well-being.

1. Purpose: <u>The Anchor</u>

Purpose provides educators with a clear "why" that steadies them in the midst of daily challenges. Purpose gives educators the stamina to deal with behavioral issues, shifting expectations, emotional demands, and the weight of supporting students who carry their own adversity. When educators understand the deeper meaning behind their work, setbacks feel less like roadblocks and more like reminders of the importance of their role.

Purpose sustains passion, fuels perseverance, and helps educators recover more quickly from stress because they know their efforts contribute to something larger than the moment. It grounds them, guides their decisions, and becomes the internal compass that keeps them steady when the work becomes overwhelming. In this way, purpose is not just motivation, it is the foundation upon which educator resilience is built.

2. Competence: The Confidence to Act

Competence helps a teacher be resilient because it strengthens confidence, reduces stress, and equips them to navigate challenges with clarity. When educators develop strong skills in instruction, classroom management, relationship-building, and problem-solving, they feel more capable of handling the unpredictable nature of K–12 environments. Competence creates a sense of mastery. Educators trust their own professional judgment and are less shaken by setbacks or difficult situations when they possess the tools necessary to deal with the myriad of situations and circumstances that await them. Instead of feeling overwhelmed, they can draw from proven strategies and past successes to adapt, adjust, and move forward. This competence also boosts emotional resilience; when teachers know they can handle it, they are more likely to remain calm, reflective, and solution-focused. Ultimately, competence provides the tools and self-assurance teachers need to withstand challenges and continue showing up effectively for their students.

3. Connection: The Protective Factor

Connection is a powerful engine of resilience for educators because it strengthens the emotional and professional bonds that sustain them through difficult seasons. When educators feel connected to colleagues, leaders, students, and the broader school community they are less likely to experience the isolation that often leads to burnout. These relationships create a network of shared wisdom where teachers can exchange strategies, process challenges, and gain perspective that helps them rebound more quickly from stress.

Connection also provides emotional grounding; having trusted people to talk with regulates stress, restores hope, and reminds teachers of their purpose. Ultimately, connected teachers feel supported, valued, and anchored, making them more capable of navigating adversity while maintaining the heart and stamina required to teach well.

4. Well-Being: *The Foundation*

Well-being is a foundational aspect of educator resilience because it sustains the physical, emotional, and mental resources teachers need to navigate the demands of the classroom. When educators prioritize their well-being, through adequate rest, healthy boundaries, emotional regulation, supportive relationships, and purposeful reflection they build the inner capacity required to respond to challenges rather than become overwhelmed by them.

An educator's well-being strengthens resilience by protecting against burnout, enhancing clarity in decision-making, and increasing the ability to adapt in moments of stress. It also fuels the patience, empathy, and composure needed to support students who may be experiencing their own adversity. Ultimately, teacher well-being is not a luxury; it is a critical component of resilient practice, allowing educators to show up with consistency, creativity, and compassion even in difficult circumstances.

Pressures That Test Educator Resilience

Every school year brings unique stressors that challenge even the most measured educators. These pressures may include:

- Rising academic and behavioral needs in a post-pandemic landscape
- Increased expectations without proportional support
- Compassion fatigue from carrying students' trauma
- Shifting policies and curriculum mandates
- Lack of resources or staffing shortages
- Navigating conflict within school communities

These realities do not indicate weakness but reveal the human cost of caregiving professions like teaching. Resilience requires acknowledging the weight of the work, not denying it.

How Resilient Educators Respond to Adversity

Resilience shows up in how educators navigate challenges. Resilient educators demonstrate:

Emotional Regulation

They stay grounded when students are dysregulated, understanding that calm is contagious.

Adaptability

They shift approaches rather than giving up, finding creative solutions to daily problems.

Reflective Practice

They ask, "What can I learn from this?" instead of "Why is this happening to me?"

Help-Seeking

They reach out to colleagues, counselors, and leadership rather than attempting to carry everything alone.

Hopeful Outlook

They maintain a belief that students can grow, situations can improve, and challenges are temporary. These behaviors are not innate as they can be taught, modeled, and strengthened over time.

School Culture as a Catalyst for Educator Resilience

Individual resilience is powerful, but it cannot flourish in an unhealthy system. Schools that promote resilience intentionally cultivate:

Psychological Safety

Educators feel safe to ask for help, try new ideas, and admit mistakes.

Restorative Relationships

Staff resolve conflict through empathy, accountability, and connection—not blame.

Supportive Leadership

Administrators communicate clearly, provide feedback, and recognize effort and growth.

Professional Autonomy

Educators have input in decision-making and flexibility in instructional strategies.

Collaboration

No one teaches alone. Teams share resources, problem-solve, and encourage one another.

When schools invest in these practices, resilience becomes a collective strength rather than an individual burden.

Why Educator Resilience Matters for Students

Student's do not learn well from adults who are overwhelmed, exhausted, or emotionally depleted. A resilient educator:

- Models emotional regulation and coping skills
- Creates a predictable, calm classroom climate
- Builds trusting relationships that become protective factors
- Maintains high expectations paired with strong support

FACING AND OVERCOMING ADVERSITY

- Demonstrates perseverance, hope, and problem-solving (skills students mirror)

When educators thrive, students thrive.

Building Educator Resilience: Practical Strategies

1. Prioritize Self-Compassion

Acknowledge limitations, celebrate small wins, and practice grace with yourself.

2. Develop a Regulation Plan

Identify strategies (breathing, mindfulness, stepping away) to restore calm during stress.

3. Engage in Reflective Practice

Journaling, coaching conversations, or peer debriefs to deepen insight and growth.

4. Strengthen Professional Community

Connection reduces burnout and expands collective resilience.

5. Advocate for Healthy Systems

Seek supports, request training, and participate in shaping school culture.

6. Maintain Purpose

Regularly revisit what brought you to education and what keeps you there.

A Closing Word: Resilience Is a journey

Educator resilience is not a finish line. It is a lifelong practice shaped by seasons, experiences, and relationships. There will be moments of strength and moments of struggle. But resilience grows when educators remain connected to purpose, supported by community, and committed to caring for themselves with the same compassion they extend to students.

A resilient educator does more than withstand adversity. They transform it, and in doing so, they become a powerful force of stability, hope, and possibility in the lives of the children they serve.

CHAPTER 9 - RESILIENCE AS A NECESSITY IN TODAY'S EDUCATIONAL CLIMATE

Teaching in an Era of Uncertainty

Today's educators stand at the intersection of unprecedented change, persistent social stressors, and escalating expectations. Schools are not simply academic institutions; they are emotional hubs, trauma-response centers, stability anchors, and spaces where hope must be cultivated daily. In such a complex ecosystem, teacher resilience is not a luxury or admirable trait—it is a professional necessity. Resilient teachers sustain their sense of purpose, remain grounded during instability, and serve as the emotional thermostat for their classrooms and school communities.

The Educational Landscape and the Pressure on Educators

Modern teaching exists within a climate defined by:

- Increased student mental health needs and trauma exposure
- Academic pressure tied to accountability, performance metrics, and policy shifts
- Societal disruptions (violence, inequity, community stressors, pandemics, technological shifts)
- Workforce instability (teacher shortages, burnout, attrition)
- Intensified emotional demands (supporting families, navigating trauma, relational repair work)

This climate can erode teacher well-being, creating exhaustion, cynicism, and detachment—conditions that directly undermine educational quality. Without resilience, educators can become overwhelmed, reactive instead of reflective, and disconnected from their "why."

Why Teacher Resilience Matters for Students

Resilience is not only about teacher survival—it directly impacts student outcomes. When teachers are well, regulated, hopeful, and psychologically present:

- Students feel psychologically safe
- Learning environments become emotionally predictable
- Instructional quality improves
- Restorative responses replace punitive reactions
- Relationships deepen
- Students learn resilience through modeling

Students learn resilience not only from curricula, but from people. A resilient teacher models' adaptability, emotional regulation, coping, problem solving, empathy, and perseverance. In many cases, the teacher becomes the clearest illustration of how to navigate adversity with dignity and strength.

Resilient Teachers Protect Their Calling and Purpose

Teaching is purpose-driven work. It requires passion, emotional investment, intellectual commitment, and relational energy. Yet purpose without resilience leads to burnout. Resilience allows educators to:

- Remain anchored in meaning despite difficulty
- Maintain hope while working with struggling students
- Rebound when lessons fail or progress feels slow
- Continue believing in students when others do not
- Stay connected to joy, humor, and humanity in the work

In essence, resilience protects the educator's heart while preserving the effectiveness of their craft.

Resilience Strengthens Instruction, Creativity, and Problem Solving

Teaching demands flexibility. Students learn differently, needs shift rapidly, and what worked one year may not work the next.

Resilient educators demonstrate:

- Cognitive flexibility – adapting instruction rather than becoming rigid
- Innovation – trying new strategies rather than giving up
- Reflective practice – learning from failure rather than internalizing defeat
- Solution orientation – focusing on what can be done

Classrooms led by resilient educators are dynamic, responsive, and intellectually alive.

Resilience Supports Trauma-Informed and Restorative Practice

Today's schools must simultaneously educate and heal. Teachers working with students facing adversity must navigate emotional outbursts, dysregulation, withdrawal, and behavioral disruptions.

Without emotional resilience:

- Teachers become reactive
- Punitive discipline increases
- Relationships are fracture
- Students internalize rejection rather than restoration

Resilient teachers, however, can remain regulated, compassionate, and consistent. They practice curiosity rather than judgment. They maintain connection even when behavior disappoints. They understand that behavior communicates need and resilience sustains the patience required to meet that need.

Teacher Well-Being is a Professional Responsibility

Teacher resilience is not self-indulgence; it is professional commitment. Schools flourish when educators flourish. Resilient teachers exhibit:

- Emotional regulation
- Healthy boundaries
- Self-awareness
- Willingness to seek support
- Commitment to continuous learning
- Capacity to recover rather than collapse

Mentally, psychologically, and emotionally "attuned" educators create well classrooms. Burned-out educators inadvertently transmit stress to students. Resilience ensures that teachers do not simply "show up," but show up with clarity, empathy, strength, and purpose.

School Culture Improves When Teachers Are Resilient

School climate is not built by policies alone—it is built by people. Resilient teachers contribute to:

- Collaborative, trusting staff environments
- Positive staff morale
- Shared problem solving rather than blaming
- Stability during change or crisis
- A culture of hope

They become emotional anchors for colleagues, team stabilizers, and leaders who foster safety and unity.

Resilience and Retention: Keeping Strong Educators in the Profession

Teacher attrition has become a national crisis. Many educators leave not because they lack skill, but because they are exhausted.

Resilience increases:

- Career longevity
- Professional satisfaction
- Commitment to the mission
- Capacity to remain in challenging schools

When resilient teachers remain, students benefit from experience, continuity, mentorship, and institutional memory.

How Teachers Build and Sustain Resilience

Resilience is not a personality trait—it is a practiced capacity. It can be strengthened through intentional habits:

1. Connection – supportive colleagues, mentors, community
2. Purpose Alignment – remembering why the work matters
3. Reflection – learning from difficulty instead of internalizing defeat
4. Self-regulation – practices that calm the nervous system
5. Healthy Boundaries – understanding that "rest is resistance" and protection
6. Professional Learning – skill building that increases confidence
7. Hope Practices – gratitude, reframing, celebrating growth

Resilient teachers do not simply endure hardship—they <u>grow</u> through it, <u>innovate</u> because of it, and <u>lead</u> in spite of it.

Resilient Teachers Build Resilient Students

Every resilient student has, somewhere in their journey, encountered a resilient adult who believed, supported, guided, and stayed in their life. In today's educational climate, teacher resilience sustains hope, strengthens instruction, stabilizes school culture, and protects the emotional health of students. When teachers thrive, students thrive. When educators remain grounded, compassionate, and resilient, they do far more than teach content—they shape lives, restore dignity, inspire perseverance, and build the next generation of resilient human beings.

Chapter 10 – Teaching Student's to Name Their Feelings and Needs

Teaching students to name their feelings and needs is foundational to emotional intelligence and resilience. When children can identify what they feel and what they need, they are better able to regulate their behavior, communicate effectively, and seek support in healthy ways. This skill doesn't happen automatically as it must be modeled, practiced, and reinforced in intentional ways.

An illustration of this skill was seen with a student/athlete I coached in Middle School. She was participating in the track & field program. This particular student came to practice on a beautiful Spring Day. She laughed and clowned with the other athletes until it was time to warm up with the team. She then vacated to the bleachers to sit down. When asked why she shrugged her shoulders saying, "I don't know coach." I pushed further hoping for a different response, and I received that response with, "Coach, I'm not sure how to say what I'm feeling and need." Also, she said, "Please don't be upset with me."

After ensuring her I would not be angry with her, that it was safe to communicate whatever she was going through, she began to cry informing me that she had not slept the night before because of her mom and dad being engaged in domestic violence. The student shared that she was feeling overwhelmed and sad, that what she needed was a safe space, and something to eat. The track team and my oversight were her safe space. Further, she knew food was available therefore, what she was feeling and needed would be provided for her.

As I move forward talking about the need for teachers to teach this skill, I'm mindful this skill is not innate; it must be nurtured intentionally through modeling, language development, and consistent practice.

Students are far more likely to express their emotions when they feel connected to the adults around them. Trust is the foundation of emotional safety, and emotional safety is the foundation of authentic communication. When students know that a teacher cares, listens without judgment, and responds with consistency and respect, they begin to feel safe enough to name what is happening inside of them.

Strong relationships create an environment where students don't fear embarrassment, punishment, or dismissal. Instead, they experience the classroom as a place where their voices matter. This sense of security encourages them to pause, reflect, and communicate openly rather than act out their emotions through behavior. For many students, especially those with trauma histories, trust must be built slowly through predictable routines, reliable responses, and genuine interest in their well-being. Over time, relationship becomes the bridge that allows students to share their feelings and articulate their needs with confidence.

Ultimately, relationship and trust are not just helpful they are essential. They clear the path for emotional honesty, reduce the emotional load students carry, and create the conditions where learning and resilience can flourish.

Building an Emotional Vocabulary

Students can only name what they have language for. Too often, children operate with a limited set of emotional words, leaving them unable to express what is happening internally. Expanding their emotional vocabulary through feeling charts, classroom visuals, and direct instruction provides them with the tools they need to articulate their inner experiences. Introducing words such as discouraged, anxious, overwhelmed, hopeful, and curious gives students more accurate ways to express themselves and reduces the likelihood of misbehavior driven by emotional confusion.

The Power of Modeling

Adults play a crucial role in demonstrating what healthy emotional expression looks like. When teachers name their own emotions and needs in real time such as, "I'm feeling a bit rushed, and I need us to transition quietly" or "I'm excited about your progress and I need your attention" then students witness emotional regulation in action. This modeling normalizes emotional honesty and teaches students that naming feelings is a sign of strength, not weakness.

Routines That Build Emotional Awareness

Emotional check-ins provide structured opportunities for students to practice self-awareness daily. Tools such as mood meters, color zones, or simple one-word check-ins help students pause, reflect, and identify their current state. When teachers follow up with questions like "What do you need to be successful today?" students begin connecting emotions to actionable needs. Over time, these routines cultivate emotional intelligence and reduce reactive behaviors.

Connecting Feelings to Needs

A critical step in emotional development is helping students understand that every feeling carries a corresponding need. Anger may indicate a need for space or fairness. Anxiety might signal a need for reassurance or clarity. Frustration may point to a need for support or more time. Teaching this connection transforms emotions from overwhelming challenges into solvable problems. Students learn to ask for what they need rather than act out what they feel.

Using Stories and Scenarios as Safe Practice

Books, role-plays, and classroom scenarios offer safe, indirect opportunities for students to analyze emotions. When students identify what a character is feeling or what a peer might need, they strengthen their ability to recognize emotions in themselves. This practice deepens empathy and builds the foundation for restorative and compassionate classroom communities.

Validation as a Pathway to Trust

Students thrive when they know their feelings will be taken seriously. Validating students such as, "It makes sense you feel that way"—creates psychological safety and reduces the shame that often drives behavioral issues. Validation does not excuse inappropriate actions; instead, it opens the door for healthier choices by acknowledging the emotional reality beneath the behavior.

Restorative Conversations That Build Skill

When conflicts occur, restorative questions help students reflect, name emotions, and articulate needs. Questions such as "What were you feeling when that happened?" and "What do you need now to make things right?" turn difficult moments into emotional learning opportunities. These conversations teach students to communicate with honesty, empathy, and responsibility.

Structured Language for Clear Expression

Providing students with sentence starters gives them the scaffolding they need to express themselves. Phrases such as "I feel ___ because ___" and "Right now I need ___ so I can ___" empower students to communicate confidently and respectfully. With consistent use, these structures become internal tools students rely on throughout their academic and personal lives.

Creating a Culture Where It Is Safe to Speak

Students will only name their feelings when the classroom environment feels emotionally safe. A culture of respect, predictable routines, and adult responsiveness will encourage students to speak openly. When students know they won't be criticized, dismissed, or punished for expressing emotions, they develop the courage to share what they truly feel and need.

Why This Matters

Teaching students to name their feelings and needs builds the foundation for resilience. It promotes self-awareness, self-regulation, stronger relationships, and reduced conflict. For students navigating trauma, stress, or adversity, this skill is not simply helpful—it is life-changing. When students learn to understand their inner world, they gain the power to shape their outer world with confidence and purpose.

Chapter 11 – Creating A Resilient Classroom Environment

Resilience is the capacity to adapt, recover, and thrive in the face of challenges. In the context of education, fostering resilience in students is not just about helping them succeed academically—it's about equipping them with the social, emotional, and cognitive skills to navigate life's inevitable difficulties. A resilient classroom environment is one where students feel safe, valued, and empowered to take risks, make mistakes, and grow from them.

Creating such an environment requires intentionality from educators. It involves cultivating strong relationships, establishing consistent routines, promoting autonomy, and embedding social-emotional learning into daily practices. In classrooms designed for resilience, students learn to persevere through setbacks, manage stress, and develop a sense of agency over their learning. The result is not only academically capable students but individuals who can face challenges with confidence, adaptability, and hope. By understanding the key conditions that foster resilience, teachers can transform their classrooms into spaces where every student has the opportunity to flourish, both as a learner and as a resilient human being.

Fostering classrooms that produce resilient students has become more important, especially since the pandemic occurred. Researchers have found that, "A useful description of the classroom conditions allowing children to succeed despite the odds can be derived from the past seven decades of developmental research on risk and resilience" (Luthar & Eisenberg, 2017; Masten, 2014, 2018; Werner, 2013).

Classroom conditions that foster resilience focus on creating a supportive, predictable, and empowering environment where students can develop coping skills, confidence, and adaptability. Here's a detailed breakdown:

1. Safe and Predictable Environment

- Physical safety: Clear rules, consistent routines, and a structured environment help students feel secure.
- Emotional safety: Students need to know they can express themselves without judgment. Teachers modeling calm, respectful behavior reinforce this.
- Predictable routines: Consistency reduces anxiety and allows students to focus on learning rather than survival.

Resilience grows best in a safe, predictable environment. When individuals know what to expect and feel emotionally and physically secure, their stress decreases and their capacity to cope increases. Consistent routines, clear expectations, and supportive relationships create stability, allowing people, especially children and students, to take healthy risks, regulate emotions, and recover more effectively from challenges. Safety and predictability do not eliminate adversity; they provide the foundation that helps individuals face it with confidence and strength.

2. Strong Relationships and Connection

- Teacher-student trust: Teachers who show genuine care, listen actively, and understand students' needs help build resilience.
- Peer support: Encouraging collaboration, empathy, and positive social interactions strengthens students' coping skills.

- Mentorship and modeling: Teachers and older peers who demonstrate problem-solving, perseverance, and self-regulation provide concrete examples of resilience.

Resilience is strengthened through healthy, supportive relationships. Trusted connections with caring adults, peers, and mentors provide emotional safety, encouragement, and guidance during times of stress or adversity. Relationships help individuals feel seen, valued, and understood along with key factors that foster hope and persistence. When challenges arise, strong relationships serve as a buffer against stress, reminding individuals that they are not alone and that support is available. In this way, connection is not just helpful to resilience—it is essential.

3. Opportunities for Autonomy and Agency

- Choice in learning: Allowing students to make decisions about tasks or projects builds confidence and a sense of control.
- Ownership of mistakes: Encouraging reflection and learning from errors fosters a growth mindset.
- Student voice: Including students in classroom decisions promotes responsibility and self-efficacy.

Resilience empowers individuals to exercise autonomy and agency by building confidence in their ability to face challenges and recover from setbacks. When people develop resilience, they learn that their choices matter and that they can influence outcomes through effort, problem-solving, and perseverance. This sense of competence encourages independent decision-making, responsible risk-taking, and self-advocacy. As resilience grows, individuals move from reacting to circumstances to actively shaping their path, strengthening both personal ownership and motivation.

FACING AND OVERCOMING ADVERSITY

4. Emphasis on Social-Emotional Learning

- <u>Emotion recognition and regulation</u>: Teaching students to identify and manage emotions supports coping under stress.

- <u>Problem-solving skills</u>: Explicitly teaching strategies to handle challenges increases adaptability.

- <u>Mindfulness and stress-reduction techniques</u>: Small practices can help students self-regulate in challenging situations.

Resilience and social-emotional learning are deeply interconnected. Social emotional learning builds the skills such as self-awareness, emotional regulation, empathy, and relationship-building those individuals need to respond effectively to stress and adversity. Resilience is the outcome of using those skills when challenges arise. As individuals practice naming emotions, managing reactions, solving problems, and seeking support, they become better equipped to adapt, persevere, and recover. Together, resilience and Social emotional learning creates a strong foundation for well-being, healthy relationships, and long-term success.

5. High Expectations with Support

- <u>Challenging yet achievable goals</u>: Students grow resilient when they face challenges with adequate support.

- <u>Feedback focused on effort</u>: Praising perseverance and strategies rather than innate ability builds persistence.

- <u>Scaffolded learning</u>: Step-by-step support helps students navigate difficulties without feeling overwhelmed.

Resilience is the bridge between high expectations and meaningful support. When individuals are held to high standards while receiving appropriate guidance, encouragement, and resources, they learn that challenges are not barriers but opportunities for growth. Support helps prevent discouragement, while high expectations communicate belief in one's ability. Resilience develops as individuals persevere through difficulty, learn from mistakes, and experience success with support. This balance fosters confidence, persistence, and a strong sense of capability with key elements of long-term growth and achievement.

6. *Inclusive and Culturally Responsive Practices*

- <u>Validation of identities</u>: Recognizing and respecting diverse backgrounds increases belonging and self-worth.

- <u>Equitable opportunities</u>: Ensuring all students can access learning and participate fully fosters resilience.

- <u>Responsive teaching</u>: Adjusting instruction to meet students' individual needs prevents repeated failure experiences.

Resilience strengthens inclusive and culturally responsive practices by honoring students' identities, experiences, and strengths as assets rather than deficits. When educators build resilience, they create environments where diverse voices are valued, cultural backgrounds are respected, and belonging is intentional. Culturally responsive practices reduce barriers to learning by fostering trust, psychological safety, and meaningful connection. This support helps students navigate adversity, develop confidence, and engage more fully. In turn, resilient learning communities empower all individuals to thrive while remaining rooted in who they are and where they come from.

7. *Opportunities to Reflect and Celebrate Growth*

- <u>Journaling or reflection</u>: Students can track progress, identify coping strategies, and recognize personal growth.

- <u>Celebrating effort and small wins</u>: Recognizing perseverance reinforces setbacks are temporary and solvable.

- <u>Storytelling and modeling</u>: Sharing examples of overcoming challenges teaches resilience by example.

FACING AND OVERCOMING ADVERSITY

I wish that every student would take the time to reflect on their journey, regardless of what grade level. Reflection allows us to recognize how far we've come, while celebration affirms that our effort mattered. When individuals pause to reflect on progress—both big and small—they gain clarity, confidence, and motivation. Celebrating growth reinforces resilience by shifting focus from perfection to progress, from setbacks to lessons learned. Together, reflection and celebration build hope, strengthen self-belief, and encourage continued growth, reminding us that development is a journey worth honoring.

In essence, a classroom fostering resilience is safe, supportive, challenging, and empowering. It balances structure with flexibility, high expectations with nurturing, and guidance with autonomy. Students leave not only academically prepared but also emotionally equipped to navigate life's challenges.

Finally, creating resilient classrooms is essential because they do more than support academic learning. They protect, stabilize, and strengthen students so they can succeed despite adversity.

Below are some key reasons, grounded in both educational practice and resilience research:

1. Students Bring Adversity into the Classroom

Many students arrive carrying:

- trauma
- chronic stress
- instability
- unmet emotional needs

A resilient classroom doesn't ignore this reality—it responds to it. It becomes a place of predictability and safety, which are foundational for learning.

Regulated students learn better.

2. Learning Cannot Thrive Without Emotional Safety

When students feel unsafe—emotionally or relationally—their brains shift into survival mode.

Resilient classrooms prioritize:

- trust
- consistency
- respectful relationships

This allows the brain to move from fight-or-flight to engagement and problem-solving.

3. Resilience Is a Teachable Skill

Resilience is not a trait students either have or don't have—it is developed.

Resilient classrooms intentionally teach:

- emotional regulation
- problem-solving
- perseverance
- healthy coping strategies

These skills prepare students not only for tests, but for life beyond school.

4. Resilient Classrooms Reduce Behavioral Issues

When students feel connected and supported:

- disruptions decrease
- engagement increases
- accountability improves

Behavior shifts from reaction to response, saving instructional time and strengthening classroom culture.

FACING AND OVERCOMING ADVERSITY

5. *Equity Requires Resilience*

Students facing poverty, trauma, or systemic barriers need schools to be protective environments.

Resilient classrooms:

- level the playing field
- reduce the impact of external stressors
- provide access to hope, structure, and support

Chapter 12 – What Resilient Students Do Differently: Profiles, Patterns, and Practices

When we look at students who thrive in the face of challenges, it's not that their lives are easier or their paths are smoother. What sets resilient students apart is what they do when life gets difficult. They experience failure, disappointment, pressure, and adversity just like everyone else—but instead of stopping, they adjust. Instead of giving up, they try again. Resilient students think differently, respond differently, and recover differently. They've learned skills, mindsets, and habits that allow them not just to survive hard moments, but to grow through them. And the powerful truth is this: resilience isn't something you're simply born with—it's something that can be taught, practiced, and strengthened in every student.

It always amazes me to watch resilient students. Whether in the classroom or on the athletic field. Witnessing a resilient 1st grader trying to open their lunchable at lunch time can be both funny and enlightening as they maneuver unwrapping the container which could take time. After a few minutes of struggle the resilient student seeks help from a lunch aide who will in turn show them the best way to open the package. This is classic resilient behavior at best all because they recognize the need for help when struggling.

Then there's the non-resilient 10th grade female who doesn't make the football cheerleading team. She storms out of the gym after not seeing her name posted on the wall as being selected. A teacher stops the student to discuss what has caused her to be angry. The student begins, with elevated voice, "I hate coach Smith because she plays favorites," "I'm better than many of the girls who tried out and where selected." When the teacher asked what the student would do next, the student shared, "Nothing." The better response would have been, "I will seek help to get better, and try again next year."

In every K–12 classroom, students respond to challenges in various ways. Some students encounter setbacks and find ways to adapt, recover, and keep moving forward, while others become overwhelmed, discouraged, or disengaged when difficulties arise. These differences are often described in terms of resilience. Resilient students are not those who avoid adversity, but those who have developed the skills, supports, and beliefs needed to navigate it. In contrast, non-resilient students may struggle not because they lack ability or motivation, but because they lack protective factors such as consistent relationships, emotional regulation skills, or a sense of hope. Understanding this distinction shifts the focus from "What is wrong with the student?" to "What does this student need to thrive?"

When tackling what resilient students do differently, I like to begin with delineating some of the differences between the resilient and the non-resilient student. Let's first look at the resilient student, then the non-resilient student.

Resilient Students

Resilient students are not defined by the absence of struggle, but by how they respond when struggle appears. What they do differently reflects learned skills, supportive relationships, and an internal sense of agency.

In contrast to students who become stuck by adversity, resilient students tend to respond in the following ways:

They interpret challenges differently.

Resilient students view setbacks as temporary and specific rather than permanent or personal. A poor grade, peer conflict, or disciplinary moment is seen as something to work through, not as a verdict on their worth or ability.

They regulate emotions instead of reacting impulsively

Rather than being controlled by frustration, fear, or anger, resilient students use coping strategies—such as pausing, naming emotions, or seeking support—to regain emotional balance and make thoughtful choices.

They persist and adjust.

When a strategy fails, resilient students are more likely to try a different approach instead of giving up. Persistence is paired with flexibility, allowing them to adapt rather than disengage.

They seek connection and support.

Resilient students recognize when they need help and are willing to reach out to trusted adults or peers. Strong relationships act as a buffer against stress and reinforce a sense of safety and belonging.

They maintain a sense of hope and purpose.

Even in difficult circumstances, resilient students believe their efforts matter and that improvement is possible. This forward-looking mindset fuels motivation and protects against hopelessness.

They take responsibility without self-blame.

Resilient students can acknowledge mistakes and learn from them without internalizing shame. Accountability becomes a pathway to growth rather than a source of defeat.

For educators, the critical takeaway is that these behaviors are taught, modeled, and reinforced. Resilience grows when schools intentionally create environments that combine high expectations with consistent support, emotional skill-building, and meaningful relationships.

Non-Resilient Students

Student's that lack resiliency often struggles to recover from setbacks and may feel overwhelmed by challenges. When difficulties arise, they may:

- View failure as a reflection of their worth or ability
- Become easily discouraged and give up quickly
- Struggle to regulate emotions such as frustration, anger, or anxiety
- Avoid challenges or disengage from learning
- Rely on negative coping behaviors or withdraw socially
- Have limited access to supportive relationships or lack trust in adults
- Feel hopeless or powerless when facing adversity

These responses are often rooted not in unwillingness, but in unmet needs—such as a lack of emotional skills, consistent support, or safe environments.

For educators, the critical takeaway is that these behaviors are taught, modeled, and reinforced. Resilience grows when schools intentionally create environments that combine high expectations with consistent support, emotional skill-building, and meaningful relationships.

Chapter 13 – Rewriting the Story: Teaching Students to Challenge False Narratives

Resilience is not only about "weathering and recovering," from adversity but also learning to recognize and rewrite the stories students believe about themselves. Many students carry internal narratives such as "I'm a failure," "I'll never succeed," "Failure is normal in my family," or "My past defines me." These false narratives inevitably shape behavior, limit effort, limit confidence, and suffocate potential. If we want resilient students, we must equip and encourage them to challenge unhealthy beliefs and replace them with truthful, empowering mindsets.

Why the Stories Student's Tell Themselves Matter

The brain naturally seeks meaning; when students don't understand why something happened, they create a story. Trauma, repeated failure, criticism, and comparison all feed negative internal scripts. Over time, these stories become lenses through which students interpret life. A resilient student isn't one without pain or difficulty. A resilient student is one who learns to question the story instead of accepting it as truth.

False narratives matter to resilience because the stories we tell ourselves shape who we believe we are. When students learn to turn difficult experiences into meaningful stories of growth rather than defeat, they build strength, understanding, and emotional coping skills. With the guidance of caring adults, children can learn to question untrue or unhelpful assumptions—about themselves, others, or situations—and reframe them into healthier, more accurate perspectives. This ability to challenge negative "made-up" stories and create more empowering ones is a powerful social-emotional skill and a core part of developing resilience.

Helping Students Name the Narrative

A false narrative must be challenged before it can be changed. Students must learn to first identify the false narrative. Educators can help students slow down and notice what they are saying to themselves when they struggle.

- "How can I help you reframe what you said about things not going your way?"
- "What conclusion have you reached about this story?"
- "If you could rename this story and give it a title, what would it be?"

Helping students name the narrative brings it out of the shadows and into the light where it can be examined with curiosity rather than shame.

Strengthening Students Ability to Ask Thoughtful Questions

Resilient students, with help from positive adults, learn to question their thoughts instead of aimlessly trusting them. It is critical that we teach students to ask leading resilience-building questions:

- Is there truth to this story, or am I feeling a certain way at the moment?
- What evidence supports this thought, and what evidence challenges it?
- Is my problem temporary or permanent?

- What would I say if my friend was experiencing this?
- Should I consider looking at this another way?

These questions retrain the brain to evaluate rather than emotionally react. Students begin to understand that thoughts are not facts—and that they have the power to reframe.

Replacing Harmful Narratives with Healthier Truths

Challenging a false narrative doesn't stop at identifying it; as the next step is to abrogate and substitute it with a healthier, realistic, and empowering narrative. We are not teaching false positivity. We are teaching grounded truth.

False Narrative: "I'm not good at History."

Resilient Narrative: "History is challenging, but with tutoring I can get better."

False Narrative: "I'm a nobody at this school."

Resilient Narrative: "It feels lonely right now, but getting connected with the book club will help me feel good about being here."

False Narrative: "I failed, so failure is how it will continue to be."

Resilient Narrative: "Failure is not the end of my story. I must keep writing my story, one chapter at a time."

This shift helps students view challenges as opportunities rather than verdicts.

Cultivating Classroom Climates That Correct Distorted Narratives

Students are more likely to rewrite harmful beliefs when they are surrounded by educators who speak life, encourage possibility, and focus on truth.

- Normalize struggle. Talk transparently about mistakes, setbacks, and growth.

- Encourage celebration when progress is achieved, not perfection.

- Model rewriting narratives. Let students hear you say, "I've had my struggles but this is how I was able to overcame."

- Challenge deficit language. When students say "I can't," respond with "Believe in yourself."

- Use stories of resilience such as Literature, history, and lived experiences as mirrors of hope.

The environment we create either reinforces false narratives or helps dismantle them.

Teaching Emotional Literacy Alongside Narrative Awareness

Students will struggle to change false narratives when they do not understand what they feel. Their inability to name their emotions like fear, shame, disappointment, frustration reduces their power. When students understand their emotional responses, they can more accurately challenge the story attached to them.

"I'm not stupid. I'm frustrated."

"I'm not angry, I am overwhelmed."

"I'm not incapable. I'm discouraged."

Language gives students a sense of control.

The Role of Caring Adults

Students rarely challenge false narratives on their own. They need caring adults who:

- See beyond behavior
- Speak to potential rather than performance
- Offer consistent encouragement
- Believe in students even when students don't believe in themselves

When students borrow an adult's belief long enough, it often becomes their own.

The Result: A Resilient Identity

When students learn to challenge false narratives, they reshape their identity and begin an upward trajectory towards destiny. They move from:

- Helplessness to agency
- Shame to self-compassion
- Limitation to possibility
- Survival to growth

Resilience grows not simply because life becomes easier, but because students learn to think differently about themselves and their circumstances. Teaching students to challenge false narratives is not just a skill—it is a gift that shapes who they become.

Chapter 14 – Growth Mindset and How It Influences Resilience

Resilient students are not immune to challenges. Many students experience setbacks, disappointment, and failure just like everyone else. It is not unusual to see students walking through the halls of Youngstown City School District who are in crisis, coming out of crisis, or getting ready to go into a crisis. Challenges are the norm for many of our students but what sets them apart is the will, determination, and desire to keep going when they want to give up. What sets them apart is not circumstance, but how they interpret and respond to challenges. One of the most powerful ways to foster this perspective is through cultivating a growth mindset.

Understanding Growth Mindset

The concept of growth mindset comes from psychologist Carol Dweck. It refers to the belief that intelligence, abilities, and skills are not fixed traits, but qualities that can develop through effort, strategies, and persistence. Dr. Dweck says, "A growth mindset is about believing people can develop their abilities" (Dweck, 2006). Dr. Dweck, further purports that, "A fixed mindset is the belief that abilities are innate and unchangeable" (Dweck, 2006).

Students with a growth mindset see challenges as opportunities to learn rather than threats to their identity. They embrace struggle, value effort, and understand that failure is part of the learning process. In contrast, students with a fixed mindset often avoid challenges, give up easily, and interpret mistakes as a reflection of their inherent ability.

Key ideas of a growth mindset

- Mistakes are opportunities to learn, not signs of failure.
- Effort is valuable, not embarrassing.
- Feedback helps improvement rather than feeling like criticism.
- "I can't do this... yet" replaces "I can't do this."

Example:

A student who fails a spelling test with a growth mindset says, "My score was not good, but I can do better."

Key Ideas of a fixed mindset

- Works to prove intelligence or talent.
- Avoids challenges for fear of failure.
- Avoids hard labor.
- Treats criticism as an attack.

Example:

A student who fails a spelling test with a fixed mindset thinks, "I'm just bad at spelling."

The Link Between Growth Mindset and Resilience

Growth mindset and resilience are closely intertwined. Here's why:

1. Persistence Through Setbacks

A growth-oriented student views failure as a temporary obstacle, not a permanent judgment. This perspective allows them to try again, problem-solve, and adapt strategies—core elements of resilience.

2. Adaptive Coping Strategies

Students with a growth mindset are more likely to seek help, experiment with different approaches, and reflect on what went wrong. They see challenges as informational, not personal, which reduces stress and fosters emotional regulation.

3. Positive Self-Talk and Narrative Reframing

Growth-minded students often engage in self-encouraging dialogue, such as:

- "I haven't mastered this yet."
- "Mistakes help me learn."
- "Effort will pay off over time."

This internal reframing strengthens resilience by replacing self-defeating thoughts with constructive, motivating ones.

4. Enhanced Motivation and Engagement

Believing that improvement is possible fuels motivation and investment in learning, even when tasks are difficult. Students become resilient not because they never fail, but because they see value in learning and growth.

Practical Strategies to Foster a Growth Mindset

1. Model Growth Mindset as an Educator

- Share personal challenges and learning journeys
- Use language that emphasizes effort and learning over innate talent
- Normalize struggle as part of the growth process

2. Reframe Failure and Setbacks

FACING AND OVERCOMING ADVERSITY

Encourage statements like:

- "What can I learn from this?"
- "This attempt is a step toward mastery."
- Use reflective prompts to help students identify lessons from mistakes

3. Celebrate Effort and Process

- Highlight persistence, strategy use, and progress rather than only grades or outcomes
- Reinforce that effort is a skill to cultivate, not a sign of weakness

4. Teach Goal-Setting and Incremental Steps

- Help students break larger challenges into achievable steps
- Track progress over time to visualize improvement
- Encourage personal reflection on growth, not comparison with others

5. Provide Feedback That Promotes Growth

- Focus on specific strategies and behaviors rather than labeling the student
- Example: "Your revision shows strong persistence and critical thinking" instead of "You're smart"

Growth Mindset Activities for the Classroom

- Reflection Journals: Students write about a recent challenge and identify what they learned.
- Success Stories: Share real-life or historical examples of individuals who succeeded through persistence.

- Mindset Language Practice: Teach students to rephrase "I can't do this" with "I can't do this yet."
- Peer Feedback Circles: Encourage constructive, growth-oriented feedback on assignments or projects.

Finally, growth mindset is more than a motivational phrase—it is a practical, evidence-based approach to nurturing resilience in students. By helping children believe in the potential to grow, we equip them to face setbacks, embrace challenges, and persist when life gets difficult. A growth mindset does not eliminate adversity, but it transforms how students respond to it, turning obstacles into opportunities for learning, growth, and stronger resilience.

Chapter 15 – Hope: Teaching Students to See Possibility

In this chapter, I will spend time communicating how hope shared can transform students' lives. Hope is one of the most powerful protective factors a student can possess. For students navigating adversity (poverty, instability, trauma, academic struggle, or fractured relationships) hope becomes the mental and emotional engine that allows them to imagine a life beyond their current circumstances. Hope doesn't erase hardship, but it reframes it. It tells students, "Your story isn't finished yet," and that belief alone begins to build the foundation of resilience.

Hope is one of the most powerful forces that shapes how individuals confront and overcome adversity. It does not erase challenges, but it transforms the way people experience them. When hope is present, adversity is no longer viewed as a permanent or defining barrier; instead, it becomes a moment in time that can be navigated, learned from, and ultimately overcome.

Hope fuels perseverance by reminding individuals that their efforts matter and that a positive outcome is still possible, even when the path is uncertain. It strengthens problem-solving by opening the mind to new strategies, supportive relationships, and creative solutions. Emotionally, hope serves as a protective buffer, reducing the weight of fear, discouragement, and despair. In many ways, hope becomes both an anchor and a compass—steadying people during the storm while guiding them toward a future brighter than their present circumstances.

Hope expands a student's sense of possibility. Adversity often narrows a child's vision until all they can see is the problem in front of them. Hope widens that vision, helping them recognize that new options, new support, and new outcomes are still within reach. When students believe that a better tomorrow is possible, they become more willing to try, to practice, to ask for help, and to stay engaged even when success feels slow. Hope fuels persistence.

Hope also strengthens a student's identity. When caring adults (teachers, counselors, mentors) speak life into children, they help them see themselves as capable, worthy, and resilient. That shift in self-perception is transformative. A student who believes "I can grow" approaches challenges with more confidence and less fear. Hope empowers them to reinterpret adversity as a temporary obstacle rather than a permanent limitation.

Equally important, hope connects students to others. It grows in relationships where belonging, encouragement, and trust are present. When a student feels supported, they learn that they do not have to face adversity alone. This sense of connection is essential for resilience because it provides stability, accountability, and emotional safety which are elements that buffer the impact of stress.

Ultimately, hope is the spark that activates resilience. It gives students the courage to move forward, the strength to endure difficulty, and the vision to see beyond the moment. Hope transforms adversity into an opportunity for growth, shaping students into young people who understand their own power, who can persevere through struggle, and rise stronger on the other side.

What is Hope? How can Hope play a major role in the lives of the children in your classrooms that you work with day in and day out? Hope can mean a lot of things to different people, though no matter how you frame it or experience it, hope is a vital aspect of our experience as human beings. Hope is always about the future. The term hope has been defined as, "Hope is the sum of the mental willpower and waypower that you have for your goals" (Snyder, 1994, p. 5). Hope can be further understood as a positive motivational state that is fueled by being positively motivated (agency) and a road map (pathways) to reach a goal.

Dr. Lopez, in his book "Making Hope Happen," shares four core prerequisites for hope that are powerful and can be useful for our students today. He says "The future will be better than the present," "I have the power to make it so," "There are many paths to my goal," "None of them is free of obstacles" (Lopez, 2013, pp. 18-19).

I define hope as, "The confident expectation of a desired outcome, based upon an inward conviction." This definition is rooted in my spiritual belief based upon Hebrews 11:1, "Now faith is the substance of things hoped for, the evidence of things not seen."

It is my hope to provide you with a perspective and practical application of hope necessary to change the narrative of lives enveloped by the despair of adversity and trauma.

- One reality that children who have suffered from adversity and traumatic experiences have in common is that they're grasping for something that will ignite hope.

- Many are hoping for change, for the despair to stop, that things will get better. Some are hoping that the turbulence, trials and tribulation will cease, that relief will manifest giving them relief/peace.

Many students, regardless of their geographic location, household make-up, and economic status face adversity. Stress, anxiety, and depression are but a few challenges which severely impact their academic achievement and healthy development. There are other social conditions, no doubt, that breed a sense of meaningless and hopelessness, which also impact their daily functioning. As result of these intractable challenges, students and those who support them, including teachers, their families, and community institutions, struggle to engage them in meaningful ways.

I must speak truth to power as the options to help our students, at times, seem few and far in between. This however, doesn't mean we must give in to the notion there's nothing else we can do to help students address and overcome their adversities. We must continue to build upon the strategies mentioned in the previous chapter to fill our "Hope Toolbox," with tools that enable us to restore hope and well-being. We can start by asking probing questions such as How do I as a teacher effectively respond to a student (s) experiencing hopelessness in ways that restore dignity, hope, and possibility? How can the responses given cause me to pursue action? What are the elements that will lead to a transformative culture and climate in my school/classroom?

I purport to you that students need a double dose of hope when they arrive in your classrooms as they may have come to school hungry, not having adequate rest due to police and ambulance sirens sounding off through the night, then having to deal with gang violence on the way home from school. Maybe, your student (s) have come in having the adversity of dealing with parents in the midst of divorce. Could it be your student (s) are facing peer pressure that's mentally and emotionally debilitating? Have you been approached by a student who informs you that they've considered, because of life's circumstances, suicide? These aforementioned situations and circumstances are but a few of the reasons helping students see the power of hope and possibility is absolutely necessary.

FACING AND OVERCOMING ADVERSITY

My grandmother, who transitioned while I was an undergraduate in college, would always encourage me. I didn't realize at that time she was teaching me to be hopeful. She would ask me to repeat saying, "I think I can, I think I can." I often remembered her words of affirmation while competing as a track and field athlete. Her words resonated with me in times of fatigue, stress, and difficulty. Saying, I think I can would prove to be the mental energy I needed to stay on schedule to meet my goals. Many of our scholars would benefit from hearing words of hope spoken to them from educators on a daily basis. The words "I think I can," should be a part of every child's vocabulary, to allow hope to usher them to a time and space of achievement, success and greatness. Christopher Reeve said, "Once you choose hope, anything's possible."

I absolutely love Bobby McFerrin's song "Don't Worry, Be Happy," and Pharrell's song, "Happy." I realize these songs are not a miraculous fix to the perplexity of adversity and traumatic events that happens in students' lives however, I do believe they convey a sense of "Collective Possibility." It is about the intentional act of gathering hope, options, and alternative pathways so that resilience can grow in the face of adversity. When students are overwhelmed or discouraged, their brain narrows its vision. Collecting possibility widens their vision again. It helps students believe, "Maybe there's another way," "Maybe things can improve." This is about curated hope.

Educators can engage in what I'm calling "Collective Possibilities." As educators, you can say, "Notice what is working," "Help students name past successes," "Reframe challenges as learning opportunities." We must build a mindset of hope by paying attention to opportunities, strengths, and potential solutions rather than the obstacles before us.

One of the most compelling illustrations of resilience can be found in the true story portrayed in movie "The Boys in the Boat." The University of Washington rowing team, composed primarily of working-class young men, rose from obscurity to Olympic victory not because they were the strongest or came from privilege, but because they learned to transform adversity into collective strength. Their journey mirrors the same resilience we strive to cultivate in K–12 students—resilience shaped by struggle, strengthened through connection, and sustained by purpose.

The story focuses on Joe Rantz, a young man who experienced profound hardship long before he ever stepped into a boat. Abandonment, poverty, and emotional instability could have defined his trajectory. Instead, rowing became a place where adversity was not a barrier but a catalyst. In the rhythm of the oars and the discipline of daily training, Joe discovered that resilience is not merely surviving difficulty but finding a way to grow through it. His persistence reflects the reality many students face and it's in the adversity that their greatest challenges often become the very ground on which their resilience is built.

The true power of the story emerges when the focus shifts from individual grit to collective resilience. What set the team apart was not physical dominance but their ability to move as one. Eight individuals synchronizing their effort, breath, and trust (A school district must collectively work together). Success demanded communication, vulnerability, and a willingness to sacrifice personal glory for shared purpose. This mirrors the classroom, where students flourish when they experience belonging, connection, and supportive relationships. Just as the crew's boat glided only when their rhythms were aligned, students thrive when the school environment is cohesive, collaborative, and grounded in mutual respect.

FACING AND OVERCOMING ADVERSITY

The team's triumph reminds educators that resilience is not only taught but modeled, nurtured, and reinforced through community. Their coaches served as mentors, encouragers, and stabilizers, helping the boys see beyond their circumstances. Likewise, educators become the steady voice guiding students toward hope when life feels uncertain. The victory at the 1936 Olympics was not simply an athletic achievement; it was evidence of what becomes possible when young people are given belief, structure, and the opportunity to rise. Ultimately, The Boys in the Boat teaches that resilience is both personal and communal. It is forged in adversity but strengthened in connection. Those young rowers learned to pull together toward a destination bigger than themselves. Our students must learn to navigate life's waters with confidence when surrounded by adults and peers who row beside them.

So, what is the hope we must give our students? It is the hope that encourages, inspires, and walks with them in their times of darkness. There will be times when life is dark, when our students are asking the question, "will I be able to overcome what I'm going through?" It is in the dark that hope allows you and I and the children we work with to see the light ahead. This is the hope we must give to our children.

Hope enables our children to say I can, I will, I must work past my situation, believing its but another transition I have to go through, climb out of, and work through. We must encourage our children to believe another day will occur, the sun will shine again, that hope allows them to see past the fog of their circumstances, catching the horizon of their future.

Hope fuels our children to get up in the morning, desiring to walk into the halls of academia, grinding day in and day out to maximize their educational potential. Hope says yes, I can, I may be down but not out, I'm more than a conqueror! Hope is the reminder of how good things can be when you reach down into the inner most part of your being past the present moment of pain, disappointment and failure to say, "my future will be better than my past."

Why Hope

It is my belief that the greatest challenge facing America today is the increasing level of hopelessness that is growing, especially in our schools. It is a hopelessness that is fueled by inequality, injustice, disparity and isolation. It is a hopelessness that we must address even in our schools. How can we begin, where do we begin, and why should we begin to embrace the challenge of practicing hope in our districts, buildings, and classrooms? When I consider hope, I do so because:

- Hope heals. Because hope can transform a traumatized child. Hope is the lifeblood of resilience.
- Hope is having that inner capacity which has been nurtured and fully developed to the point of conviction. True hope is that inner conviction and determination that will cause you to keep moving forward even while the darkness shields your eyes from the light that everything inside tells you is just around the bend.
- Hope, is having that internal capacity to see no obstacle or challenge as being greater than you.
- Hope builds resilience. True hope can look any momentary setback in the eyes and say with conviction…I will!!

Fostering hope in your students:

As educators, parents, and coaches we have the responsibility to teach and instill hope in the students we are entrusted with. Why? Because hope should be an essential ingredient in the development of children. It is a tool that ultimately allows our students to navigate life's challenges. With the news, social media, and every day real-life situations enveloping young people with despair, tragedy, and death, we must make every effort to find ways to share positivity, joy, and hope. Here are a few ways to impact students with hope:

1. Visually exhibit an attitude of hope
2. Allow your students to take ownership over their accomplishments
3. Remind your students those challenges are life lessons
4. Verbalize your students potential and effort

I close this chapter with some powerful but practical strategies to help k-12 students develop hope and see possibility:

1. Teach a "Possibility Mindset" Through Language

Students learn possibility through the word's adults use.

Replace "I can't" with "I can't yet."

Use sentence starters such as:

- "What's another way we could approach this?"
- "What might be possible if…?"
- "What would success look like for you?"

Why it works: Language shifts the brain toward creative, expansive thinking instead of limitation.

2. Strengthen Students' Sense of Personal Agency

Give students structured opportunities to make real choices:

- Let them select project topics.
- Allow choice in learning pathways.
- Invite them to co-create classroom norms.

Why it works: Agency fuels hope. When students feel their actions influence outcomes, they can imagine new futures.

3. Model "Possibility Thinking" as an Educator

Students watch what teachers believe more than what they say.

- Share stories of your own challenges and how you discovered options.
- Verbalize your thinking when you hit a tough moment:
- "This didn't work—we need another strategy. Let's brainstorm."

Why it works: Your transparency teaches them that solutions exist—even when they are not immediate.

4. Use Future-Oriented Visualization Activities

Have students:

- Write letters to their future selves.
- Map out "one-year goals," "one-month goals," and "one-week actions."
- Draw a "future version" of themselves with strengths and achievements.

Why it works: Visualization activates hope pathways and helps students test-drive possibility.

5. Celebrate Progress, Not Perfection

Praise:

- Effort
- Creativity
- Strategy use
- Courage to try new things

Why it works: Students learn that growth is possible even when outcomes are not perfect.

6. Teach Students to Reframe Adversity

Introduce reframing questions:

- "What is this challenge trying to teach me?"
- "What strength am I using right now?"
- "How might this help me in the future?"

Why it works: Reframing builds resilience by turning setbacks into stepping stones.

7. Surround Students with "Possibility Examples"

Use:

- Stories of individuals who overcame adversity.
- Classroom displays highlighting student achievements.
- Quick case studies of young innovators, survivors, creators, and changemakers.

Why it works: Representation builds belief.

8. Incorporate Collaborative Problem-Solving

Provide group tasks that require creativity:

- Build challenges
- Open-ended projects
- Design thinking lessons

Ask:

- "How many solutions can your group come up with?"

Why it works: Multiple approaches teach students that there is rarely only one way forward.

9. Teach Students to Name Their Strengths

Use strengths assessments or simple sentence frames:

- "One strength I see in myself is…"
- "A strength others notice in me is…"

Why it works: Students who know what they bring to the table can imagine new opportunities.

10. Replace "What's wrong?" with "What's possible?"

At moments of frustration, teach a simple pivot:

- Instead of asking "What's the problem?" ask:
- "What's possible right now?"
- "What's one small next step you can take?"

Why it works: Students learn to shift from problem-focus to possibility-focus.

I conclude this chapter with words from Dr. Lopez who says, "Hope matters," "Hope is a choice," "Hope can be learned," "Hope can be shared with others" (Lopez, 2013, p. 13).

"In fact, hope is best gained after defeat and failure, because then inner strength and toughness is produced." (Fritz Knapp, May 10, 2020).

Chapter 16 – From Struggle to Strength: How Students Grow Beyond Adversity

Adversity is what we experience when life gets hard, unfair, overwhelming, or uncertain. Also, adversity becomes a place where resilience can be developed. Adversity is not the end of a student's story; for many, it becomes the moment their story begins to change. Students do not simply "bounce back" from hardship—they grow forward when the right supports, environments, and personal strengths converge. Thriving beyond adversity is not accidental; it is the result of connection, skill building, hope, and intentional guidance.

There are many types of adversity students will face. There is personal adversity such as family illness, grief from death, and self-doubt. Social adversity can manifest in ways such as bullying, exclusion, even identify challenges. The environment plays a role in adversity. Students who come from impoverished backgrounds, unsafe neighborhoods, and unstable living conditions are impacted. Then there are academic adversities like learning gaps, pressure to achieve, and discouragement. Traumatic adversity can rear its ugly head by way of abuse, violence, and chronic stress.

What I believe, have seen, and stand on is that adversity does not automatically break our students. Yes, it tests, shapes, and with the right support strengthens them. It becomes a defining place where resilience character, and perseverance are formed.

Thriving Begins with Connection

The most consistent predictor of thriving after adversity is a caring relationship with a trustworthy adult.

Students flourish when someone consistently communicates:

- You matter.
- You are capable.
- You are not alone.

The aforementioned affirmations are important to students who are becoming resilient. As they, not only build connection, but enable students to hear from those they are connected with and believe to be an integral part of their lives.

Affirmation is more than kind words—it is an intentional act of speaking truth, value, and possibility into someone's life. For students facing pressure, doubt, or adversity, affirmation becomes a stabilizing force that shapes identity, confidence, and hope. When caring adults communicate, "I see you. I believe in you. You are capable of greatness," affirmation interrupts negative self-talk, counters shame-based narratives, and replaces fear with belief.

Affirmation strengthens the brain's emotional pathways connected to confidence and perseverance. It helps students internalize messages of worth and ability, shifting their mindset from "I can't" to "I can try" and eventually to "I can succeed." Consistent, authentic affirmation builds resilience because it reminds students that failure is not final, mistakes are not identity, and struggle is not a measure of their worth. Over time, affirmed students develop stronger self-regulation, clearer purpose, and a deeper sense of belonging

Teachers, counselors, parents, mentors, and coaches become anchors during turbulent seasons. These relationships stabilize emotions, restore confidence, and remind students that they are valued beyond their circumstances. Belonging is not optional—it is protective.

Mindset Transforms Struggle into Growth

Students thrive when they develop a resilient mindset—the belief that challenges can shape, not shatter, their future.

They learn to reinterpret adversity:

- Setbacks become temporary.
- Failure becomes feedback.
- Struggle becomes strength-building.

This mindset shifts students from helplessness to agency. Instead of asking, "Why is this happening to me?" they begin to ask, "What can I learn from what I'm going through? How can I grow from what I've experienced?" The way students think about adversity determines how they respond to it. The connection and affirmation that students receive from any adult is laudable. Affirmation takes the connection further. When adults speak truthful, specific encouragement into a student's life, it shapes identify and mindset.

Ultimately, it is laudable because it is both morally right and educationally powerful. It honors student's humanity while equipping them with courage, resilience, and self-worth. Connection and affirmation do not simply help students feel good, it helps them become stronger, healthier, and more capable of reaching their maximum potential.

Emotional Regulation Builds Internal Strength

Thriving students learn how to manage overwhelming feelings. They are taught how to name emotions, understand what they are experiencing, and use healthy coping strategies—breathing techniques, movement, reflection, journaling, conversation, or prayer. Emotional awareness does not erase adversity, but it strengthens the nervous system and improves focus, behavior, and decision-making. Students who can regulate emotions are better equipped to persist academically and socially.

Imagine a middle school student named Jason. During class, he receives a lower grade on an assignment he worked hard on. He feels frustrated and disappointed—his heart beats faster, his face feels warm, and negative thoughts begin to swirl. But instead of reacting impulsively, Jordan practices skills he has learned.

He takes a slow breath to calm his body. He quietly reminds himself, "I'm upset right now, but I can handle this." Instead of slamming his notebook or shutting down, he asks to speak with his teacher after class. When they talk, Jordan expresses his feelings respectfully: "I was really disappointed with my grade. Can you help me understand what I need to improve?" Together, they review his work, identify ways to grow, and he leaves with a plan rather than a meltdown. It is clear that Jason, because of being able to regulate his emotions, exhibits internal strength. Jason's internal strength will serve him, not only in the classroom, but in every facet of his life.

Purpose Fuels Persistence

Students who thrive beyond adversity have a reason to keep going. Purpose may come from faith, family, mentors, personal goals, or a vision of the future. Purpose gives pain meaning and transforms endurance into determination. Hope becomes a powerful protective factor—not blind optimism, but a grounded belief that effort matters, tomorrow can be better, and they have a role in shaping it.

Over the course of many years in education, I've seen many students, regardless of their grade, wondering about aimlessly. The adversities of life have affected them and they have not considered their life purpose (who they want to become, where they want to go, how to get where they want to go). The phrase "Without vision, people perish" speaks to what happens when individuals live without direction, meaning, or a sense of where their lives are headed. When applied to students, it paints a powerful picture: students who live without purpose often do not physically perish, but they can emotionally, academically, and motivationally diminish. Without vision, they <u>drift</u> rather than <u>drive</u>. They may disengage from school, stop believing their effort matters, and lose hope that their future can be meaningful. A lack of purpose leads to apathy, poor decision-making, and vulnerability to negative influences because nothing compelling is pulling them forward.

Purpose, on the other hand, gives students something to reach toward. It fuels motivation, strengthens resilience, and helps them endure adversity. When students have a vision for who they can become and why their life matters, they show greater persistence, better emotional health, stronger academic engagement, and deeper hope. Vision anchor's identity and directs behavior. In short, just as people "perish" without vision, students shrivel inwardly without purpose—but with it, they come <u>alive</u>, <u>strive</u>, and <u>thrive.</u>

Skill Development Turns Hope into Capacity

Thriving is not only emotional; it is practical. Students need opportunities to develop:

- problem-solving
- self-discipline
- communication
- academic competence
- perseverance

Success—no matter how small—creates momentum. Each accomplishment strengthens identity and reinforces a powerful internal message: "I can do hard things." In other words, hope is the motivation, and skill development is the mechanism that allows motivation to translate into achievement. For example, a student may hope to graduate or succeed in a sport or art form, but only by practicing, learning strategies, and applying effort does that hope become actual progress.

Skill development transforms potential energy (hope) into kinetic energy (capable action), enabling students not just to dream about the future, but to actively shape it.

Supportive Schools Help Students Rise

Students thrive when schools intentionally create environments that support resilience. Resilient schools:

- provide psychological safety
- pair high expectations with high support
- foster inclusivity and belonging
- empower student voice and agency
- teach social and emotional skills

Systems either crush resilience or cultivate it. When schools choose empathy, structure, compassion, and high standards, students gain the conditions they need to rise. A critical question for every educator, administrator, and stakeholder is: "Is my school a supportive school that helps students rise?" Supportive schools do more than deliver curriculum—they create environments where students feel seen, valued, and capable. They provide structure without rigidity, high expectations paired with high support, and opportunities for students to learn, grow, and recover from setbacks.

FACING AND OVERCOMING ADVERSITY

Asking this question forces us, as educators, to examine whether our school actively cultivates resilience or merely reacts to problems. Are students encouraged to take risks and learn from failure? Do they have trusted adults who guide, affirm, and challenge them? Are social-emotional needs prioritized alongside academics?

Rewriting the Narrative

Ultimately, thriving beyond adversity is about story.

Students begin to rewrite internal narratives from:

- "I'm broken" → "I am becoming stronger."
- "I can't change my future" → "I have influence and possibility."
- "This defines me" → "This refines me."

When students learn to rewrite their story, they move from seeing themselves as victims of circumstance to authors of their future. Every student has a story—but not every student has been taught that they can rewrite it. The narratives students tell themselves about who they are, what they are capable of, and what their future holds can either limit them or set them free. When students begin to replace false or limiting beliefs with truths about their effort, growth, and potential, transformation begins. They can say, "Our past may have shaped us, but it does not have to define us."

Rewriting a narrative doesn't erase challenges or mistakes—it reframes them. A student who once thought, "I'll never succeed," can learn to say, "I am learning, growing, and capable of more than I imagined." With guidance, affirmation, and resilience-building strategies, students can shift from feeling powerless to feeling empowered, turning setbacks into lessons and hope into action.

Chapter 17 – The Need for Resilience-Based Interventions for Students

Student's today navigate an increasingly complex world marked by academic pressure, family stressors, social comparison, trauma exposure, community violence, and ongoing uncertainty. These adversities do not impact all students equally; those affected by poverty, discrimination, unstable home environments, or chronic stress are disproportionately impacted. Without intentional support, many young people begin to internalize failure, develop negative identity narratives, disengage from school, and experience emotional and behavioral challenges that hinder learning.

Resilience-based interventions are essential because they move beyond simply reacting to student problems and instead proactively build the internal strengths and external supports students need to thrive. Grounded in resilience science, these interventions help students develop protective factors such as self-regulation, problem-solving, emotional awareness, hope, purpose, and adaptive coping. Equally important, resilience work strengthens relationships with caring adults, fosters belonging, and creates school environments where safety, affirmation, and connection are the norm. When students believe they matter and have the skills to navigate difficulty, they are far more likely to persist, learn, and succeed.

Schools are uniquely positioned to deliver resilience-building supports because students spend a significant portion of their developmental years within school communities. When resilience-based practices are embedded into classrooms, counseling programs, restorative practices, and school culture, they do more than help students "bounce back." They equip students to grow through adversity, build healthy identities, remain emotionally regulated, and pursue meaningful futures. Ultimately, resilience-based interventions are not optional enhancements; they are essential tools for ensuring equity, humanizing education, and supporting student well-being and long-term success.

Without intervention, youth facing significant adversities have a greater likelihood of encountering problems as they navigate their developmental paths (Luthar & Cicchetti, 2000). A key idea is that interventions need to focus on developing assets and resources for those exposed to risk rather than concentrating on risk amelioration (Fegus & Zimmerman, 2005; Luthar & Cicchetti; Yates et al., 2003).

In the past, practitioners focused on documenting predisposing, enabling, and reinforcing factors associated with youth's behavior targeted for change (Fergus & Zimmerman). Typically, deficits are highlighted that predispose, enable, and reinforce negative behaviors; however, a resilience approach emphasizes assets and resources as the center for change. Interventions cutting across behaviors may be the most effective due to the multidimensional nature of resilience. Furthermore, intervention strategies must be tailored to the student's developmental level (Noam & Hermann, 2002).

Moving Beyond a Deficit Lens

Education settings can help move students beyond academic deficit. For too long, education systems have been dominated by deficit thinking. Students struggling behaviorally or academically are labeled "unmotivated," "defiant," or "problem students" (Skiba et al., 2014). This mindset has historically pathologized student behavior, particularly among students from marginalized communities.

Traditional disciplinary responses often punish the symptoms of trauma and stress rather than addressing the root causes. Students are sent away, suspended, or labeled as "behavior problems," when in reality, many are communicating pain they do not yet have the emotional vocabulary to express.

Resilience-based interventions intentionally shift this paradigm. They operate from a strengths-based lens that sees possibility rather than limitation. Instead of asking, "What is wrong with this student?" resilience-centered educators ask, "What has this student experienced, and what support do they need to thrive?" This shift honors student dignity, reinforces belonging, and positions educators as partners in healing rather than being enforcers of compliance.

Research shows that when educators adopt a strength-based, trauma-responsive mindset, student engagement increases, behavior improves, and trust deepens (Brunzell et al., 2018). Resilience-based thinking reframes behavior as communication and invites compassionate intervention rather than exclusion.

Schools serve as primary environments for fostering Resilience Building

Schools are uniquely positioned to foster resilience because they are one of the most stable, predictable environments many children experience. Students spend thousands of hours in classrooms during their formative years. This gives educators an extraordinary opportunity—not only to teach content, but to help shape emotional competence, identity, and coping capacity.

When resilience-based practices are woven into school systems, they do more than respond to crises; they create cultures where:

- connection is prioritized over control

- regulation is valued over reaction
- restoration is preferred over punishment
- affirmation replaces shame
- and belonging interrupts isolation

Elementary School Resilience Interventions:

Emotional Regulation - Breathing exercises, mindfulness moments, emotion naming, calm-down corners, feelings charts

Primary Outcomes - Improved self-regulation, reduced meltdowns, emotional awareness

Emotional Literacy - Morning meetings, storybooks on emotions, role-play of feelings, puppetry

Primary Outcomes - Increased understanding of emotions, empathy, expression skills

Social Skills Development - Friendship lessons, sharing practice, turn-taking activities, cooperative games

Primary Outcomes - Stronger peer relationships, fewer conflicts

Predictable Safety & Structure - Visual schedules, consistent routines, positive classroom management

Primary Outcomes - Safety, trust, emotional stability

Growth Mindset Foundations - Encouragement phrases, effort praise, celebrating small wins, learning-from-mistakes activities

Primary Outcomes - Confidence, resilience mindset, perseverance

Family Engagement - Parent communication, family partnership meetings, take-home coping resources

Primary Outcomes - Home–school consistency, support network

Early Restorative Practices - Simple restorative circles, "repair the hurt" conversations, apology and reflection guidance

Primary Outcomes – Accountability with care, relational healing

Middle School Resilience Interventions:

Emotional Regulations & Stress Skills – Coping skills lessons, grounding strategies, journaling, movement breaks

Primary Outcomes – Reduced anxiety, improved impulse control

Identity & Belonging – Advisory programs, student voice groups

Primary Outcomes – Positive identity, peer inclusion, self-worth

Peer Support & Relationships – Peer mentoring, small groups, social skills groups

Primary Outcomes – Decreased isolation, improved connection

Growth Mindset & Academic Resilience – Teaching failure as learning, goal-setting, reflection tools, study resilience strategies

Primary Outcomes – Motivation, persistence, academic engagement

Restorative Justice Practice – Restorative circles, harm repair processes, alternatives to suspension

Primary Outcomes - Reduced conflict, strengthened community trust

High School Resilience Interventions:

Advanced Coping & Stress Management – Cognitive coping skills, stress workshops

Primary Outcomes – Lower anxiety, emotional maturity, healthier coping

FACING AND OVERCOMING ADVERSITY

Purpose, Hope, & Future Orientation – College & career mentoring, goal planning

Primary Outcomes – Motivation, hope, direction, agency

Identify, Voice & Empowerment – Culture identity affirmation, student leadership councils

Primary Outcomes – Empowerment, dignity, positive identity

Life Skills & Resilience Competence – Decision-making lessons, real-world problem solving, resilience curriculum integration

Primary Outcomes – Independence, competence, readiness for adulthood

Restorative & Trauma Response Systems – Restorative conferencing, re-entry support, wraparound services

Primary Outcomes – Reduced suspensions, healing & accountability

Chapter 18 – Profiles in Resilience

The Story of Justus Uwayesu

When we talk about resilience, we are not speaking of convenient inspiration or glossy motivation. We are speaking about a strength born in unthinkable places—where survival itself feels uncertain. Few stories illustrate this truth more clearly than the journey of Justus Uwayesu.

Justus was a child of Rwanda's devastating 1994 genocide, a tragedy that took his parents, fractured his sense of security, and thrust him and his siblings into a life defined by scarcity and fear. With nowhere safe to call home, childhood for Justus did not unfold in classrooms, playgrounds, or places of warmth. Instead, it led him to the outskirts of Kigali—to a garbage dump—where he slept inside the shell of a burned-out car and survived by scavenging.

Yet even in an environment where most young children focus only on getting through the day, Justus carried something remarkable inside him: vision. One day, when humanitarian workers visited the dump searching for children to help, many asked for food, clothing, or money. But when they asked Justus what he wanted most, he did not ask for temporary relief. He answered with uncommon clarity:

"I want to go to school."

That single request—simple yet profound—became the turning point of his life. Education became his doorway out of despair. Once given the opportunity, Justus did not merely attend school; he excelled. He learned languages, rose to the top of his classes, became a student leader, and developed a deep conviction that his success should lift others as well. His determination propelled him to global recognition and ultimately to Harvard University—an outcome almost unimaginable considering where his journey began.

But Justus's story is not simply about personal achievement; it is about transformation with purpose. Rather than distancing himself from his past, he used it as fuel to support others still facing adversity. He helped provide school supplies, financial assistance, and encouragement to vulnerable students, proving that resilience is not only the capacity to rise—it is the willingness to reach back and pull others up.

What Students Learn from Justus

Justus's story teaches students and educators powerful truths:

- Resilience begins with vision. Even when life strips everything else away, the ability to name a future worth striving for is powerful.

- Education is more than academics; it is liberation. Access to learning can reshape identity, restore hope, and redirect destiny.

- Support systems matter. Resilience strengthens when determined young people meet compassionate adults who open doors.

- Purpose deepens resilience. The strongest form of resilience is not merely overcoming hardship—it is transforming hardship into service.

Why This Story Belongs in Our Classrooms

When students encounter Justus's journey, they witness resilience not as theory but as lived reality. They see that hardship does not define destiny. They discover that determination, belief, opportunity, and compassion can change a life—and that they, too, possess the capacity to persevere, choose growth, and impact others.

Justus Uwayesu's life stands as a living testimony: adversity may shape the beginning of one's story, but it does not have to dictate the ending. His journey reminds us that resilience is both a mindset and a mission—a commitment to hope, a dedication to learning, and a promise to ensure that rising is never done alone.

The Story of Ludwig van Beethoven

When we speak of resilience, we often imagine courage in the face of circumstances that challenge physical endurance or emotional strength. But sometimes adversity attack's purpose itself. For the great composer Ludwig van Beethoven, adversity came for the very gift that defined his identity—his hearing.

Beethoven did not begin life with privilege or ease. Raised in a troubled home with an alcoholic father and little stability, his childhood was marked by harsh pressure and emotional turmoil. Music became the place where he found meaning, voice, and a sense of belonging in the world. By his early twenties, Beethoven had earned recognition as one of Europe's most promising young musicians. His gift was undeniable. His future appeared certain.

Then, the unthinkable happened. Beethoven began to lose his hearing. The decline was slow—a faint ringing, muffled conversations, sounds slipping just beyond clarity. But as months turned into years, the loss became permanent and devastating. For a musician, hearing is not a luxury; it is oxygen. Silence threatened not only his career but his identity, dignity, and purpose. In despair, Beethoven withdrew socially, battled depression, and even questioned whether life still had meaning. The world around him grew quieter, colder, and more isolating.

Yet within that darkness, a remarkable decision emerged. Rather than surrender to silence, Beethoven refused to allow his disability to define him. He chose to keep composing, even though he could no longer hear the music he created. He began to "hear" sound internally—through memory, emotional intuition, and imagination. He pressed forward not because the path was easy, but because his calling mattered. His adversities did not weaken his artistry; they deepened it. Out of profound struggle came some of the most emotionally powerful compositions the world has ever known.

Beethoven composed his Ninth Symphony—one of the greatest musical masterpieces in history—while completely deaf. When it debuted, the audience erupted in thunderous applause, but Beethoven could not hear it. He stood facing the orchestra as the hall shook with celebration. Only when a musician gently turned him toward the crowd did he see the overwhelming response. In that moment, applause replaced the silence he had lived with for so long—not in sound, but in recognition of the indomitable spirit behind the music.

What Students Learn from Beethoven

Beethoven's journey teaches students powerful truths about resilience:

- Resilience means refusing to be defined by limitation. Even when something precious is taken away, purpose can remain.

- Adversity can deepen creativity and strength. Hardship does not always shrink our capacity; sometimes it stretches it.

- Persistence is not denial of pain—it is choosing meaning despite it.

- True greatness is not the absence of struggle; it is what rises from within it.

Why His Story Matters for Today's Students

Student's today face emotional challenges, learning struggles, discouragement, trauma, and moments when they feel unheard, unseen, or overwhelmed. Beethoven's story reminds them that even when life alters a dream, it does not erase potential. Resilience does not always mean returning to life as it was; sometimes it means courageously redefining what is possible.

Beethoven's life echoes a profound message: adversity may change the conditions of our journey, but it does not have to silence our purpose. His legacy teaches us that resilience is not only endurance—it is transformation.

The Hidden Figures Story

Resilience is often forged quietly—far from recognition, applause, or public praise. The true story portrayed in the film Hidden Figures reveals resilience lived out in perseverance, brilliance, and dignity by three extraordinary women: Katherine Johnson, Dorothy Vaughan, and Mary Jackson. Their story teaches students that resilience is not only about surviving hardship, but about excelling in the face of injustice and opening doors for others to follow.

Set during the early days of NASA's space program, these three African American women worked as mathematicians and engineers at a time when both racial segregation and gender discrimination shaped daily life. They were often excluded from meetings, denied opportunities, and forced to work harder simply to be seen as equal. Yet they refused to allow discrimination to define their worth or limit their contributions.

Katherine Johnson demonstrated intellectual resilience. Her extraordinary mathematical ability helped calculate flight trajectories critical to America's space missions, including John Glenn's historic orbit of Earth. Even when her work was questioned or dismissed because of her race or gender, Katherine stood firm in confidence, competence, and quiet determination. Her resilience was rooted in excellence.

Dorothy Vaughan embodied leadership resilience. When she realized her department was being phased out due to technological changes, she did not resist progress—she mastered it. Dorothy taught herself and her team computer programming, ensuring their relevance and securing future opportunities not only for herself, but for the women she led. Her resilience lifted others as she rose.

Mary Jackson modeled advocacy resilience. With dreams of becoming an engineer, Mary faced legal and institutional barriers that prevented her from taking required courses. Rather than surrender, she petitioned the court for permission to attend an all-white school. Her courage opened doors, allowing her to become NASA's first Black female engineer and later an advocate for inclusion.

What Students Learn from the Women of Hidden Figures

Their collective journey teaches enduring lessons:

- Resilience thrives in excellence. Doing one's best can challenge unjust systems.
- Barriers do not define ability. Talent, determination, and preparation matter.
- Leadership includes lifting others. True resilience creates pathways, not walls.
- Advocacy is a form of courage. Speaking up changes systems.

Why This Story Matters for Today's Students

Student's today face obstacles that may feel invisible to others—bias, discouragement, self-doubt, or lack of opportunity. The women of Hidden Figures show that resilience is not always loud or confrontational. Sometimes it is steady, faithful, brilliant work done with dignity and perseverance.

Their legacy reminds us of a powerful truth: when resilience is combined with courage, knowledge, and unity, it has the power not only to change individual lives, but to alter the course of history.

The Liz Murray Story

Some stories remind us that resilience isn't born in comfort, but in the determination to rise when life feels impossible. The story of Liz Murray, often known as "Homeless to Harvard," stands as a powerful reminder that even in the most destabilizing circumstances, hope can take root, vision can grow, and a future can still be rewritten.

Liz grew up in New York City in a home marked by addiction, instability, and emotional pain. Both of her parents struggled with substance abuse. While other children returned to homes filled with routine, guidance, and structure, Liz returned to one marked by uncertainty, hunger, and chaos. Her childhood was not defined by opportunities but by survival.

School quickly faded from priority as life at home unraveled. By her early teens, Liz found herself without a stable place to live. After her mother died from complications related to AIDS and her father became unable to care for her, Liz became homeless. She slept in stairwells, on friends' couches, and on subway trains. She had every reason to give up. Many people in similar circumstances disappear into statistics.

FACING AND OVERCOMING ADVERSITY

Liz refused to let her life end in hopelessness. Standing on the edge of her circumstances, she made a decision that would change everything: she returned to high school—while homeless. Carrying her belongings in a bag, often exhausted and unsure where she would sleep at night, Liz chose education as an anchor. She completed four years of high school in just two years, earning top grades while navigating the daily trauma of homelessness.

Her resilience drew the attention of educators who believed in her potential. With the help of mentors and scholarship opportunities, Liz applied to Harvard University—**and she was accepted**. It wasn't a fairy-tale ending, but it was a powerful turning point. Liz **didn't** simply escape her past; she transformed it into purpose. She went on to share her journey globally, inspiring countless students, families, and educators with a message grounded in courage, dignity, and determination.

What Students Learn from Liz Murray

Liz's journey offers profound lessons for students and educators alike:

- Resilience is a daily decision. It is choosing hope again and again, even when circumstances say otherwise.

- Education can be a lifeline. School became stability, belonging, and possibility when life offered none.

- Support systems matter. Teachers, mentors, and compassionate adults help hold students when life is too heavy to hold alone.

- Your story does not define your future. Background does not equal destiny.

Why Her Story Matters for Today's Students

Many students silently carry trauma, instability, grief, and fear into classrooms every day. Liz Murray's story shows them that struggle does not disqualify them from greatness. It reminds educators that behind every disengaged face may be a story of survival—not laziness. Most importantly, it affirms that resilience is not perfection; it is persistence fueled by hope.

Liz Murray's life embodies a powerful truth: adversity may shape our beginnings, but resilience empowers us to rewrite the ending. Her journey reminds us that potential can survive hardship, purpose can rise from pain, and when compassion meets determination, extraordinary transformation is possible.

The Nelson Mandela Story

There are some lives that remind us that resilience is not only about enduring hardship—it is about transforming suffering into strength, anger into purpose, and injustice into a call to create a better world. Few leaders in history embody this kind of resilience more powerfully than Nelson Mandela.

Mandela was born in South Africa during a time when the system of apartheid stripped Black citizens of dignity, rights, and freedom. From a young age, he witnessed inequality not as something distant or theoretical, but as a daily reality shaping every aspect of life. Instead of accepting the world as it was, Mandela chose to become a voice for justice, equality, and human dignity.

That choice came at a cost. Mandela was arrested, separated from his family, labeled a threat, and eventually sentenced to life in prison. He spent 27 years behind bars, much of it in harsh conditions—breaking rocks, sleeping on a thin mat, and being allowed only limited visits and letters from loved ones. Prison could have broken his spirit, fueled bitterness, or silenced his hope.

Mandela made a different choice. Inside prison, he disciplined his mind and guarded his heart. He committed himself not to hatred, but to purpose. He studied, reflected, and strengthened his leadership. Rather than allowing prison to make him smaller, he allowed it to deepen his wisdom, strengthen his compassion, and sharpen his resolve. He once wrote that while jail could restrain his body, it could not restrain his belief in justice.

When Mandela was finally released after nearly three decades, the world expected revenge. Instead, Mandela chose reconciliation. He helped guide South Africa toward democracy, unity, and healing, becoming the nation's first Black president. He did not erase the truth of injustice, but he refused to let bitterness dictate the future. His resilience was not only survival—it was moral courage.

What Students Learn from Nelson Mandela

Mandela's journey offers profound lessons about resilience for students and educators:

- True resilience is rooted in purpose. When you stand for something meaningful, you can endure great hardship.

- Adversity can shape character rather than destroy it. Struggle can strengthen clarity, courage, and integrity.

- Forgiveness is a powerful expression of resilience. It takes strength to move forward without allowing anger to own your future.

- Leadership and resilience go hand in hand. Standing firm in values, even when it is costly, transforms communities—not just individuals.

MARTIN FREEMAN

Why His Story Matters for Today's Students

Student's today encounter injustice, discouragement, conflict, and moments when life feels unfair or overwhelming. Mandela's life teaches them that resilience is not passive—it is active, principled, and hopeful. It reminds them that strong character, patience, and commitment can outlast even the harshest circumstances.

Nelson Mandela's legacy teaches a defining truth: resilience is not just the capacity to endure hardship—it is the courage to rise from it with dignity, compassion, and purpose. His story reminds us that while adversity may shape our journey, it does not have to define our spirit.

The Florence Chadwick Story

Resilience is not only about strength; it is about vision—the ability to keep going when what you're reaching for is not yet visible. Few stories illustrate this more powerfully than the journey of Florence Chadwick, one of the world's greatest long-distance swimmers, whose life teaches students that sometimes the greatest barrier isn't the storm around us, but the doubt within us.

Florence Chadwick was no stranger to challenge. From an early age, she trained not in calm swimming pools, but in open water—where waves crash unpredictably, waters turn icy, and conditions constantly change. She dreamed not merely of swimming for medals, but of pushing human limits.

In 1952, Florence set out to swim from Catalina Island to the coast of California—a 26-mile swim through frigid water, strong currents, and heavy fog. As she swam, the fog grew so dense she could not see the coastline ahead. For hours she battled exhaustion, numbness, and uncertainty, unsure how much farther she had left. Surrounded by fog, unable to see success, worn down by fatigue, Florence finally

FACING AND OVERCOMING ADVERSITY

stopped. She was pulled from the water. Only then did she learn the truth that she was less than one mile from the shore.

Later, reflecting on the moment, Florence said, "I'm not excusing myself, but if I could have seen the land, I know I could have made it." The barrier wasn't her strength. It wasn't the cold. It wasn't the distance. It was the fog.

Two months later, Florence returned to the same waters. The same cold. The same currents. The same physical pain. Only this time, she carried something different: a mental picture of the shore. Even though the fog was just as thick and she still could not see land, she kept reminding herself that the coastline was there. This time, she finished the swim.

Florence didn't just complete the journey—she set a world record, proving that when vision is stronger than discouragement, resilience prevails.

What Students Learn from Florence Chadwick

Florence's story powerfully reminds students and educators:

- Resilience requires vision. When you can't see the finish line, belief must carry you.
- Failure does not define you; it prepares you. Florence didn't quit her dream—she returned stronger.
- Mental resilience is as important as physical strength.
- Hope is a skill. Sometimes progress doesn't feel visible, but it is still happening.

Why Her Story Matters for Today's Students

Student's face "fog" all the time—uncertainty about academics, emotions, family challenges, grief, identity, and the future. They often grow discouraged not because they lack ability, but because they cannot "see" results yet. Florence Chadwick's story teaches them that resilience means believing in what you cannot yet see, trusting the process, and refusing to quit when life gets cloudy.

Her journey reminds us of a powerful truth: resilience is not just enduring the storm; it is holding onto the vision beyond it. When determination and hope stand stronger than doubt, ordinary people accomplish extraordinary things.

The Chaz Freeman Story

Yes, this is the story of my son. The son of Martin and Marshell Freeman.

Resilience is not only found in history books, heroic legends, or famous figures. Sometimes resilience lives closest to our hearts—in the quiet strength of those we love. The story of Chaz Freeman is one such powerful testimony. His life reminds us that resilience is not the absence of hardship, but the determination to keep living with purpose, joy, and faith when life changes without permission.

At age 35, when many people are settling into the familiar rhythms of adulthood, building careers, raising families, and planning futures, Chaz received a life-altering diagnosis: Multiple Sclerosis (MS). MS is not a short-term challenge. It is a lifelong condition that brings uncertainty, physical challenges, emotional weight, and moments of fear that cannot always be seen by others.

For many, a diagnosis like this can feel like the closing of doors—dreams paused, strength questioned, identity shaken. But Chaz chose a different response. Rather than allowing MS to define the boundaries of his life, he continued to define his life by passion, calling, and love. Today, Chaz is a professor of Writing at Rutgers University, shaping minds, guiding students, and continuing to do what he loves—teaching, thinking deeply, lifting others, and contributing meaningfully to the world of education. His diagnosis did not silence his voice. It did not steal his brilliance. It did not stop his purpose.

Even more beautifully, Chaz is not only a scholar and educator—he is a husband and father of three boys (Cristian, Cross, Cebastien). His wife Christa (also a special education teacher), has been his constant – his encourager, his anchor, and a steady presence reminding him he is never fighting alone.

His life is not defined by limitation, but by love, laughter, purpose, and presence. His resilience is not loud or theatrical. It shows up in everyday courage—showing up for his family, showing up for his students, showing up for himself.

Chaz's story reminds us that resilience is deeply human. It is waking up on days when the body feels heavy and choosing gratitude anyway. It is having every reason to retreat, yet continuing to participate fully in life. It is living with faith, hope, intelligence, humor, and dignity, even when the road is steep.

What Students Learn from the Story of Chaz Freeman

Chaz's journey speaks powerfully to students and educators:

- Resilience is not "getting over" something, but living well in the midst of it.
- Purpose gives strength. When you know why you live, you find the courage to continue.
- Family, community, and love matter. Support strengthens resilience.

- Adversity does not erase identity. You are still gifted. Still capable. Still called.

Why His Story Matters

For students who face health challenges, chronic conditions, invisible struggles, or unexpected life changes, Chaz's life testifies that their story is not over. Life may bend, but it does not have to break. Dreams may be challenged, but they do not have to disappear.

The story of Chaz Freeman teaches a profound truth: resilience is not just about surviving—it is about continuing to live with meaning, purpose, and heart. His life stands as a reminder that even when adversity walks beside us, hope, strength, and love can still lead the way.

Allow me to conclude with a spiritually rooted message of resilience. In seasons of strength and seasons of struggle, keeping God first anchors the heart in something greater than circumstances. When life feels uncertain, God provides stability. When challenges feel overwhelming, He offers peace that human strength cannot supply. Placing God first does not mean life becomes easy; it means we never face life alone. It shifts our perspective from fear to faith, from control to trust, from self-reliance to divine guidance.

Keeping God first reminds us that purpose does not end when adversity appears. It ground's identity not in what happens to us, but in who God says we are—loved, valued, capable, and never forgotten. It shapes decisions, strengthens character, deepens resilience, and fuels hope when emotions run empty. In every victory and every valley, prioritizing God keeps the soul centered, the mind steady, and the heart courageous.

To keep God first is not merely a spiritual discipline; it is a lifeline. It is choosing to trust His plan, lean on His grace, and believe that

FACING AND OVERCOMING ADVERSITY

even in difficulty, He is working, sustaining, and building in each of us resilience.

Acknowledgements

I am deeply grateful to Superintendent Jeremy Batchelor for his valuable input and encouragement, the educators, leaders, parents, and students who inspired the vision behind this work. Special thanks to the district Scholar Advocates and Social Workers for their insight and partnership throughout this journey. At every staff meeting, I would hear the need as to why I should write this book. Heartfelt appreciation for my colleague and Pastor Garrick Matlock who heard my passion, and saw my tears writing this book. Thank you, Shaunda Yancey who reviewed my drafts for this manuscript. Finally, I thank my family for their patience, love, and unwavering belief in me.

ABOUT THE AUTHOR

Martin Freeman (B.A., MABTS, Th.D., LSW) has served in Social Work, Education, and ministry for over 30 years.

Martin is currently employed with Youngstown City Schools where he serves as District Ombudsman. He has received the District Administrator or the Year Award in 2023, and the Anthony DeNiro Distinguished Service Award in 2024. Martin is a National Conference and motivational speaker.

Martin loves education, ministry, enjoys teaching, family, children, and is an avid golfer. Martin is the Author of his first published book "The Quest for Contentment," and his second book titled, "Incites to Excite: Inspiration for Everyday Living."

REFERENCES

Alvord, M. K., & Grados, J. J. (2005).Benzies & Mychasiuk, 2009; Fergus & Zimmerman, 2005; Martinez-Torteya, Bogat, von Eye, & Levendosky, 2009; Masten et al., 1991; Rak & Patterson, 1996; Walsh, 2003).Enhancing resilience in children: A proactive approach. Professional Psychology: Research and Practice, 36(3), 238–245, http://dx.doi.org/10. 1037/0735-7028.36.3.238.

Bandura, A. (1997). Self-efficacy: The exercise of control. New York, NY: W.H. Freeman.

Bath, H. (2008). The three pillars of trauma-informed care. Reclaiming Children and Youth, 17(3), 17–21.

Bath, H. (2008). Brunzell, T., Stokes, H., & Waters, L. (2016). Trauma-informed positive education: Using positive psychology to strengthen vulnerable students. Contemporary School Psychology, 20(1), 63–83.

Bethel CD, Newacheck P, Hawes E, Halton N. Adverse childhood experiences: assessing the impact on health and school engagement and the mitigating role of resilience. Health: Aff. 2014; 33 (12): 2106-2115. doi: 10.1377/dhlthaff.2014.091

Block, A. (2021). 5 Factors That Promote Resilience. Anti-Poverty Service-Learning Resources, University of Nebraska Omaha. https://digitalcommons.unomaha.edu/antipoverty/15.

Bhatnager, S. (2021). Rethinking stress resilience. *Trends in Neuroscience*, 44 (12), 936-945. https://doi.org/10.1016/j.tins.2021.09.005

National Scientific Council on the Developing Child. (2015). *Supportive relationships and active skill-building strengthen the foundations of resilience.* (Working Paper No. 13). Center on the Developing Child, Harvard University.

Compas, B., Jaser, S., Bettis, A., Watson, K., Gruhn, M., Dunbar, J., et al. (2017). Coping, emotion regulation, and psychopathology in childhood and adolescence. Journal of Child Psychology and Psychiatry, 58(4), 321–349.

Durlak, J., Weissberg, R., Dymnicki, A., Taylor, R., & Schellinger, K. (2011). The impact of enhancing students' social and emotional learning. Child Development, 82(1), 405–432.

Dweck, C. S., (2006). Mindset. The New Psychology of Success. New York, NY: Random House.

Esch, P., Bocquet, V., Pull, C., et al. (2014). The downward spiral of mental disorders and educational attainment. Social Psychiatry and Psychiatric Epidemiology, 49, 129-139.

Fergus, S., & Zimmerman, M. A. (2005). Adolescent resilience: A framework for understanding healthy development in the face of risk. Annual Review of Public Health, 26, 399–419,
http://dx.doi.org/10.1146/annurev.publichealth.26.021304.144357

Furlong, M., O'Brennan, L., & You, S. (2011). Psychometric properties of the California school climate survey. Journal of Psychoeducational Assessment, 29(4), 273–287.

Garmezy, N. (1991) a. Resilience in children's adaptation to negative life events and stressed environments. Pediatric Annals, 20, 459-460, 463-466.4.

Goleman, D., (1995). Emotional Intelligence: Why it can matter more than IQ. New York, NY: Bantam Books.

Gwinn, C., & Hellman, C. (2018). Hope Rising: How the Science of Hope Can Change Your Life. Morgan James Publishing.

Hattie, J., & Timperley, H. (2007). The power of feedback. Review of Educational Research, 77(1), 81–112.

Jennings, P. & Greenberg, M. (2009). The prosocial classroom. Review of Educational Research, 79(1), 491–525.

Lopez, S. J., (2013). Making Hope Happen: Create the future you want for yourself and others. New York. Free Press.

Luthar, S. S., & Cicchetti, D. (2000). The construct of resilience: Implications for interventions and social policies. Development and Psychopathology, 12, 857–885.

Masten, A. S. (2001) Ordinary magic: Resilience processes in development. American Psychologist. 56, 227-238

Masten, A. S. (2014). Global perspectives on resilience in children and youth. Child Development, 85 (1), 6-20.

National scientific council on the developing child. (2015).

Noam, G. G., & Hermann, C. A. (2002). Where education and mental health meet: Developmental prevention and early intervention in schools. Development and Psychopathology, 14, 861–875

Perry, B. (2006). Applying principles of neurodevelopment to clinical work with maltreated children. In N. Boyd Webb (Ed.), Working with traumatized youth in child welfare.

Perry, B., & Szalavitz, M. (2006). The boy who was raised as a dog: And other stories from a child psychiatrist's notebook. New York, NY: Basic Books.

Rutter, M. 2006. Implications of resilience concepts for scientific understanding. Annals of the New York Academy of Sciences, 1094, 1-12.

Shonkoff, J. P., et al. (2012). The lifelong effects of early childhood adversity and toxic stress. Pediatrics, 129(1), e232-e246. https://doi.org/10.1542/peds.2011-2663

Skiba, R., Arrendondo, M., & Williams, N. (2014). Organizing for change in school discipline. Review of Research in Education, 38(1), 245-27

Snyder, C. R. (1994). The psychology of hope: You can get there from here. New York: Free Press.

Snyder, C. R. (2002). Hope theory: Rainbows in the mind. Psychological Inquiry, 13(4), 249–275. https//doi.org/10.1207/S15327965PLl1304-01

Sammons, P., Day, C., Kington, A., Gu, Q., Stobart, G., & Smees, R. (2007). Exploring variations in teachers' work, lives and their effects on pupils: Key findings and implications from a longitudinal study. British Educational Research Journal, 33(5), 681-701. https://doi.org/10.1080/01411920701582264

Southwick, S. M., Charney, D. S., Depierro, J. M., (2023). Resilience. The Science of Mastering Life's Greatest Challenges (p. 3)

Walsh, F. (2003). Family resilience: A framework for clinical practice. Family Process, 42(1), 1–18.

Weir, K. (2017, September, 1st). Maximizing Children's Resilience. Monitor on Psychology, Vol. 48. No 8. P. 40).

Werner, E. E. 1982. Vulnerable, but invincible: A longitudinal study of resilient children and youth. American Journal of Orthopsychiatric Association, 59.

Werner, E., & Smith, R. (2001). Journeys from childhood to midlife. Cornell University Press.

Yeager, D., & Dweck, C. (2012). Mindsets that promote resilience. Educational Psychologist, 47(4), 302–314.

Zimmerman, B. (2002). Ungar, M., (2015). Becoming a self-regulated learner. Theory Into Practice, 41(2), 64–70.*

www.ingramcontent.com/pod-product-compliance
Lightning Source LLC
LaVergne TN
LVHW052234110526
838202LV00095B/222

Anger Management

The 21-Day Mental Makeover to Take Control of Your Emotions and Achieve Freedom from Anger, Stress, and Anxiety

PUBLISHED BY: James W. Williams

Copyright © 2019 All rights reserved.

No part of this publication may be copied, reproduced in any format, by any means, electronic or otherwise, without prior consent from the copyright owner and publisher of this book.

James W. Williams

Table of Contents

Your Free Gift 5

PART 1: Anger – A Cry for Help or a Desire to Control? .. 6

Day 1: What is Anger? 7

Day 2: Signs and Symptoms of Anger 14

Day 3: Why Do I Get Angry? 21

Day 4: Anger in Children 27

Day 5: Anger in Teens 36

Day 6: Anger as Part of Grief 43

Day 7: How Anger Affects Relationships 51

Day 8: Anger in the Workplace 59

Day 9: Anger-Related Disorders 66

Day 10: Anger Across Cultures 72

PART 2: Anger Management 77

Day 11: When Anger Becomes a Problem 78

Day 12: Handling Emotions 87

Day 13: Emotional Intelligence and Anger Management 95

Day 14: Emotional Intelligence 102

Day 15: Mindfulness 109

Day 16: Meditation 117

Day 17: Zen Buddhism and the Importance of Living in the Present..127

Day 18: Inner Peace Techniques for Anger Management...133

Day 19: Cognitive Behavioral Therapy 140

Day 20: Nutrition for Stress Relief....................................... 150

Day 21: Putting It All Together..157

Thank you 164

Your Free Gift

As a way of saying thanks for your purchase, I wanted to offer you a free bonus E-book called **Bulletproof Confidence,** exclusive to the readers of this book.

To get instant access, just go to:

https://theartofmastery.com/confidence/

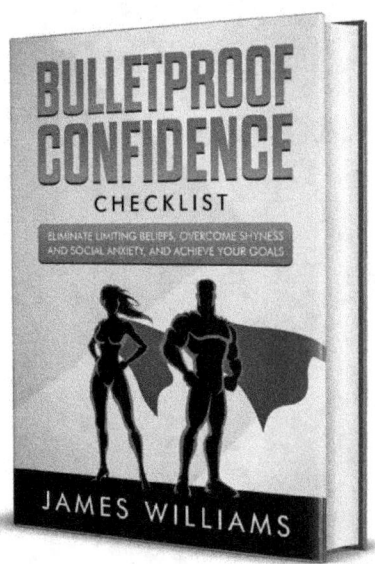

Inside the book, you will discover:

- What are shyness and social anxiety, and the psychology behind them
- Simple yet powerful strategies for overcoming social anxiety
- Breakdown of the traits of what makes a confident person
- Traits you must DESTROY if you want to become confident
- Easy techniques you can implement TODAY to keep the conversation flowing
- Confidence checklist to ensure you're on the right path of self-development

PART 1

Anger – A Cry for Help or a Desire to Control?

Day 1

What is Anger?

Anger as a Powerful Emotion

Anger is a feeling we are all familiar with, although we experience it and express it in different ways. The usual cause of anger is a reaction to an unfair decision or treatment, as well as to criticism, being embarrassed in public, being bullied, feeling impatient, somebody's rude behavior, being ignored, losing, being dumped, and many more unpleasant experiences.

However, while anger is a perfectly natural part of life, it's not something we should encourage. On the contrary—most people try to control their anger, especially in social situations. Perhaps there were times in the distant past when being openly angry was a crucial survival skill, but in the sophisticated and densely-populated world we now live in, different survival techniques will help you succeed.

Like with so many other things in life, there are two sides to anger—it can be both a positive and a negative force in your life. On the upside, anger often serves as a sign that things are not right and that something needs to be done about the situation, like if you are facing unfair treatment, having to deal with rude people, or standing in a queue for too long. However, we often make ourselves angry by having unrealistic expectations.

Anger Management

The downside of anger, especially out-of-control anger, includes a long list of behaviors that lead to ruined relationships, domestic violence, imprisonment, destroyed health, spoiled opportunities, and more.

Often, the so-called primary anger masks the emotions that are the real reason for our aggression. The most common secondary emotions leading to anger are fear—often manifested as anxiety and worry—as well as sadness, because of a real or imaginary loss.

The reason these feelings cause anger is that fear and sadness make people feel vulnerable or threatened, and to stop themselves from becoming overwhelmed with these emotions, people often shift into anger mode. A friend of mine once said that it was only when she was behaving aggressively that she felt truly alive.

By shifting your fear of being dumped by your partner into anger, you subconsciously give yourself a shot of adrenalin, which makes you feel energized and in charge rather than helpless and vulnerable.

If used positively, this boost of energy can actually help you get out of a tricky situation or find a better resolution to a problem. However, if creating this false sense of confidence and control over the situation means you actually become aggressive and start abusing others, the adrenalin rush that created this powerful feeling will probably create more problems rather than offering any solutions.

Self-Anger

Turning your anger and frustration inward, whether you are aware of it or not, is one of the most self-destructive things you can do to yourself.

If you're angry with yourself for not being more attractive, more successful, or happily married, start by asking yourself what's stopping you from getting what you want. If you stay with this question for a while, you'll realize that you either don't really want these things or that the effort of getting them would outweigh any benefits you'd see.

Unfortunately, not having what you'd like or think you deserve is often the result of choices you made in the past which you are now paying for—wrong life partner, wrong investment decision, remaining in a dead-end job, and so on.

Not having what you want is a complicated issue, especially if the reason you can't get something is beyond your control, as things often are. Although having dreams can be a powerful motivating force that can help you overcome setbacks, having unrealistic dreams or not doing enough to make them happen will only make you sad, resentful, and—worst of all—angry at yourself for not having tried harder.

We usually turn anger outward, to other people—like the government, a particular person, or even life in general. However, those who turn their anger inward, toward themselves, usually reach a point where it manifests as self-hatred or rejection of certain aspects of self that they believe are a cause of their failure in life. So, like how in extreme situations, anger can lead to murder, self-anger can similarly lead to suicide.

Anger comes in many disguises—as resentment, ranting and raving, or blame. But it can also be masked by such feelings like impatience, envy, guilt, or low self-esteem.

So, what to do if you are openly or secretly angry at yourself? Besides learning anger management, you can do one of two things.

<u>2 things to do when feeling angry at yourself:</u>

- **Forgive yourself**

    Your failure to be what you think you should be or have what you think you deserve could be due to wrong life choices, or simply unrealistic expectations. However, while acknowledging your mistakes is necessary before you can move forward, beating yourself up over something you did or failed to do will get you nowhere. Instead of wallowing in your guilt or self-hatred, learn from your mistakes, face your demons (guilty thoughts, hurt feelings, disappointment) and stop replaying over and over again in your head that you're a failure. If you can forgive others, why can't you forgive yourself?

- **Work out why you're angry**

    If the reason for your anger is justified, do something about it. If it isn't, don't stress yourself by constantly thinking about how unfair life is, how ungrateful children can be, how selfish, rude, or arrogant people are.

If you think you deserve better and believe you can use your anger to make others aware of the injustice done to you, doing what you think may improve the situation.

However, don't forget that anger often breeds more anger, as well as resentment and fear. To prevent self-destructive behaviors and thoughts, stop thinking about the past (and your failures) and shift your focus to the present (and new opportunities).

Learn to Understand Your Anger

Before you try to control your anger, you have to make sure you understand what is causing it—what is REALLY causing it.

Next time you feel angry, try to calm down so you can think clearly about what's making you mad. This is not easy and you'll probably need to try more than once, because we often become masters at fooling ourselves.

<u>4 steps in understanding your anger:</u>
   1. **Acknowledge your anger**

      Stop telling yourself (and others) "I'm fine." You can't be fine if deep down you are seething with rage.

Unless you acknowledge you have a problem, you won't be able to start looking for a solution.

2. Identify the key feeling behind your anger

This can be tricky, but if you are used to tuning into your emotions, it won't be too difficult. Emotional intelligence is a tool that can help you understand your emotions, and why your anger often masks more intense emotions such as disappointment, loneliness, or abandonment.

3. Ask yourself why

Once you work out what really fuels your anger, be brutally honest with yourself and admit why the fear, sadness, envy, or any other secondary emotion is making you so upset. For example, you may fear the future (if you believe you will be made redundant soon), you may fear loneliness (if you suspect your partner is contemplating leaving you), you may fear death (if you know you have a serious health issue), you may feel sad (because you let someone down), you may feel resentful (because of missed opportunities), you may feel envious (because amongst all your friends, you are the only one still living with your parents).

4. Deal with the secondary emotion

There are issues that can be resolved, and those that are beyond your control. If your anger stems from something that can be changed or improved, work on addressing this so you can close that chapter of your life and move on.

If your anger is caused by a secondary emotion, like fear, guilt, or anxiety, you should find a way to express this feeling in a healthy way.

When you understand what your anger is actually about, it will become much easier to find a way to deal with it. Although figuring out what is making you angry will not make the anger go away, it will at least help you keep it under control.

Anger is a very powerful emotion. The trick is to use its energy as fuel to motivate yourself to improve your life and get where you want to be.

Food for Thought:

1. Think of a time when you were very angry. Try to remember how you felt, how you looked, and how you behaved at the time. Do you think your reaction was justified? How would you react in the same situation today?

2. List three things that make you most angry. Why?

3. How do you react when you witness an angry outburst in public? Do you pretend not to see or hear anything? Do you try to get as far away as fast as you can? Or do you try to find out what's going on?

Day 2

Signs and Symptoms of Anger

When You Can Feel it Coming

ome people get angry very easily. Some might stay angry for days or months, while others can let go of built-up tension through an angry outburst, then simply forget about it and move on—though this doesn't mean those around them can do the same.

Certain people may decide to do nothing about their anger, and instead hold on to it for years, until such a time when they can no longer take it and an angry scene follows. Although many anger-related issues cannot be resolved, the worst thing you can do is let your anger turn into bitterness, be it about life in general or about a particular person or incident.

After an angry outburst, you may feel relieved because you let go of accumulated tension, but it can also make you feel flat, embarrassed, or foolish—not to mention the stress you've created for those who had to witness the scene.

In any case, there are warning signs one is about to "explode." We all learn to recognize these signals from an early age, and continue to perfect the skill as we grow up. Just like we are taught that a dog is getting ready to attack if it flattens its ears, we learn how our parents look or behave when they are mad by watching how they react when they realize we've done something we shouldn't have. Later in life, we learn to interpret the subtle—or not so subtle—signs our partner is about to leave us, or we're about to be laid off.

Being able to pick up vibes from your environment and understand what's going on even when nothing is said is a very useful skill which can sometimes be a real lifesaver.

The tell-tale signs you, or someone else, is about to become angry and possibly dangerous are many, and vary from person to person. However, some of them are common and easy to notice.

16 traits of people prone to anger and/or aggression:

1. They frequently experience road rage.
2. They often blame others for their misfortune.
3. They often feel threatened and believe that others are out to get them.
4. They make scenes when angry.
5. They get angry for even small and insignificant things.
6. They use dominating body language, threats, and screaming to control others.
7. They easily lose their temper.
8. They easily become frustrated.
9. They are unable to control themselves even when they know they'll be sorry later.
10. They have a history of domestic violence.
11. They are in chaotic or problematic relationships.
12. They refuse to accept they have anger issues.

13. They often think or boast about violent confrontations with others.
14. They have been arrested for violence.
15. They drink excessively and are aggressive when drunk.
16. They believe and boast they can easily make others do what they want.

If you know that you or someone close to you is experiencing anger issues, the best thing to do is to explore various anger management techniques which could help not only deal with an explosive temper but understand what it is that makes someone react in such a way.

How Does Being Angry Make You Feel, Look, and Act?

Some people are quick to anger, either because they are short-tempered or because they feel entitled to certain things. Others may need more time to get upset, but their anger may be longer lasting. However, the most problematic type of anger is the kind that leads to physical violence.

Anger is a powerful emotion which affects us on both a physical and emotional level. It not only invokes a strong physiological response, often leading to aggressive and destructive behavior like shouting, thrashing, or violence, it also changes our emotions and encourages certain behaviors we may later not even remember.

Blind rage is particularly common when people are set off for one of these three reasons:

- **Major loss** - For example, a stolen car, a broken-into apartment, or a bag snatched in a restaurant.
- **Grief** - For example, your best friend killed by a drunken driver, your partner cheats on you with someone you trusted.
- **Humiliation** - For example, being belittled in front of others, being insulted because of the way you look, being bypassed for promotion.

While anger can lead to aggression, there's also a positive side to this emotion—it often makes you take steps you might not have otherwise. These steps often lead to change, which does not always have to be external: if you've been bypassed for promotion, you may decide it's time to look for another job, or if your apartment regularly gets broken into, you may decide it's time to improve on security or move to a safer neighborhood.

If you've been angry for years, it may be a sign that something within you needs to change, such as your beliefs, goals, needs, or priorities.

Whether anger will have a negative effect on your life or health, or whether it will prompt you to look deep within and make positive changes in your life, will depend on how honest you are with yourself and how willing you are to embrace change.

Most people who have an anger issue know very well they have a problem, but few decide to do anything about it. If left unaddressed, anger can not only make you a social outcast, but may lead to broken relationships, lost friendships, and even imprisonment.

Anger is like an adrenaline shot which, if not occurring often or allowed to get out of hand, can actually boost your confidence and sense of self-worth. A "dose" of anger, especially if you are fighting for the right cause, can make you feel strong and self-aware.

Just like animals exhibit certain behavior when facing an enemy—dogs raise the fur on their back, cats flatten their ears, horses stamp the ground—people also change their appearance when feeling threatened.

When angry, people may also display some of the behaviors used by many animals. Based on the fight-flight-freeze theory, if they decide they will neither flee nor freeze, but choose to fight, people will often stand tall with slightly spread arms, showing they are ready to fight. They may shout, thrash, or stamp their feet to demonstrate how angry they are, they could become red in the face which makes them look fierce, or they may stare at the opponent or point a finger at him. These body language signals are all part of atavistic behavior, which has helped us survive and which is understood across cultures.

Not only do angry people look threatening, the adrenalin rush makes them feel strong and ready to charge. And when you look and feel threatening, it's easy to go a step further and behave violently.

Physical reaction when feeling angry:

- Increased heart rate
- Increased blood pressure
- Increased breath rate
- Hormonal changes (adrenalin rush)
- Muscles become tense (ready to hit or receive a blow)
- Face becomes red (because of increased blood pressure)

Anger can take different paths and can invoke different emotions, from a desire for physical confrontation to severing communication and withdrawal from the situation or the person you're angry with. However, the physical and emotional manifestations of anger rarely happen at the same time, but are usually spread over a certain period.

How we react to anger depends on our personality, how emotionally intelligent we are, as well as on what caused the anger. Still, certain reactions seem to be common among angry people.

9 stupid and counterproductive things people do when angry:

1. Use bad language
2. Drink excessively
3. Throw or break things
4. Threaten others
5. Refuse to listen
6. Cry
7. Say things they don't mean

Anger Management

8. Behave as if they are entitled to whatever they want
9. Feel proud for demonstrating their strength even over much weaker opponents

So, if you know you're prone to feeling angry, and especially if you often act aggressively, the best thing to do is to start anger management treatment. You can either seek professional help, or you can try to help yourself by reading suitable self-help materials or attending an anger management course.

Anger takes many forms and people deal with it, or struggle with it, in different ways and with different levels of success. However, if you know you've felt angry for a long time, don't assume you're used to it and can continue to deal with it on your own. Bottled-up emotions can change the way you think and behave, even without you realizing it, so it's best to do address it before the accumulated resentment gets you into trouble.

Food for Thought:

How do you usually react when angry? Do you later regret it?

Do you think letting go of bottled up emotions by shouting and screaming at others is okay as long as the person feels less tense afterward?

Some claim that mental or emotional abuse is as bad, or even worse than physical abuse. Do you agree?

Day 3

Why Do I Get Angry?

Many things affect how often you get angry, how long you stay angry, and how you express your anger. Although we all have different anger thresholds, they usually revolve around feelings of personal safety and self-image.

Causes of Anger

Our anger is often based on our interpretation of the situation we find ourselves in. But how we react in a situation also depends on our triggers for anger, which vary from person to person and usually have something to do with our personal boundaries or our view of justice.

<u>4 most common triggers of anger:</u>

1. Feeling threatened
2. Feeling "cornered," helpless, or desperate
3. Feeling you are not being treated fairly
4. Facing injustice (yours or others')

However, we are all different—not everyone may feel threatened, provoked, or mistreated in the same situation. The way we react to challenges has a lot to do with who we are. Our experiences, both those we are currently going through as well as those we went through in the past, affect how we react in a situation, or with people who remind us of something or someone that made us feel unpleasant. The more troubled our life is, the more likely we are to be emotionally unstable, and the greater our need for anger management skills will be.

<u>4 factors that influence your reaction in a challenging situation:</u>

- **Your background**

    If you grew up in a family where it was okay to show your emotions, you will likely continue to be open about your feelings, both positive and negative, as an adult. However, this also means that if you were spoiled as a child and managed to get what you want by throwing tantrums, you will probably continue to exhibit similar behavior throughout life.

    If you were brought up believing that it's rude to complain, chances are you worked out how to swallow your pride and hurt early on. The trouble with this attitude is that unless you later learn how to express your anger, there is a danger you may turn it inward, on yourself.

    And if you witnessed a lot of family violence, you likely grew up believing that anger is a terrifying feeling, and will try to avoid any kind of confrontation for fear of provoking violence.

- **Your past experiences**

  If there are past experiences, like childhood abuse or bullying, that you didn't deal with, you are probably still trying to cope with those feelings of anger even though you may not be aware of it. So, even if you appear happy and confident, deep down, you may still be fighting demons from the past. As a result, you might find certain situations or people difficult to deal with, and if you can't avoid them, being around them is likely to make you feel angry—even though no one would understand why you feel this way.

- **Your current circumstances**

  If you are going through a tough time at the moment, facing a divorce, redundancy, serious health issue, or the loss of a loved one, you are probably not quite yourself. As a result, you probably get angry easily, though you may not understand why.

  If there are situations that you find personally challenging or threatening and you don't address them, the unresolved issue may find an outlet in angry outbursts—which may happen when you least expect it.

  Also, if you are grieving for someone, you may be overwhelmed by conflicting emotions such as sadness, anger, sense of emptiness, guilt, and so on. These contradictory feelings may make it very difficult to cope with otherwise normal challenges, and this may affect how you relate to those you come in contact with. For example, you may snap at others, burst into tears for no reason, or have brief episodes of unexplainable rage.

- **Possible health issues**

  Sometimes, certain health issues may be the cause of anger. According to the mind-body doctrine, our emotions and physical health are very closely linked and depend on each other much more than we realize. Anger can have neurological triggers and if you can't stop feeling angry, or you come to a stage where you wake up feeling angry, you should seek professional help as soon as possible.

  Anger may also be caused by chronic exhaustion. If you are feeling constantly tired, you will have much less energy to do what you're supposed to, or may find it more difficult to concentrate and persevere with your tasks. For these reasons, you'll most likely be less successful in life which, in turn, may make you feel angry with yourself.

Personal Judgment as a Leading Cause of Anger

How we go through life has a lot to do with our mindset—our values, what we see as right or wrong, what we experience as injustice, how cooperative we are, and so on.

Based on this, it makes sense that our own judgment about a situation will decide if we experience it as a threat or injustice. Basically, it is how WE see the world and what WE think is the right reaction to certain triggers and challenges.

It follows that anger, as an emotional response, is about how we experience reality.

So, if you perceive that a situation justifies an angry response, you will act accordingly. This often means that you may decide to take justice into your own hands, which is how many unnecessary confrontations happen.

If you are struggling with anger issues, try to get to a stage where, before you act or react, you can stop for a moment and look at the situation (an argument, provocation, a stupid joke) from a different angle. Try to see it from someone else's eyes. Give the person who is making you angry the benefit of the doubt. What if your judgment is wrong? What if you are overreacting?

We often react based not on facts, but on what we THINK is happening. And what we think is usually influenced by our experiences, culture, and temperament. This is why insight— our ability to have an accurate understanding of a situation or a person—is so important. And so is good judgment, especially when trying to understand what's going on and make the best decision.

However, many studies show that anger does cloud your judgment, which means it's important to calm down before making any big decisions—especially if you know you have a short temper. A recent study published in the academic psychology journal *Intelligence* suggests people prone to anger are also those most likely to overestimate their intelligence, particularly their ability to make good decisions.

Scientists from the University of Warsaw found a link between quick temper and a slightly skewed perception of intelligence. And this is not because these people are not intelligent, but because anger triggers the release of stress hormones that change the way your brain works. In other words, you need to either learn to control your anger or refrain from making any major decisions until you have calmed down.

Food for Thought:

Do you easily get angry? If you do, what are your main triggers? If you don't, how do you control your temper in challenging situations?

1. If memories of how your ex treated you make you "see red," how can you prevent this past hurt from affecting your future relationships? How often do you get angry because something reminds you of a wrong someone has done to you in the past?

2. Do you hate yourself after arguing with someone, or do you pat yourself on the back because you "showed them"?

Day 4

Anger in Children

Just like anger is a perfectly normal emotion in adults, it is equally normal in children. However, there is a major difference between an occasional tantrum or meltdown and prolonged or intense anger outbursts that can lead to ugly scenes or even harm to self or others.

Why Do Children Get Angry?

When anger in children occurs occasionally and passes quickly, we can assume it's part of growing up. But if it becomes an outburst of very intense emotions that last for a long time, it can easily be a mask for an anger-related health disorder.

Dealing with angry children can be difficult, as most parents will testify. Not only is it exhausting both physically and mentally, it sometimes leaves parents feeling guilty or ashamed if they overreacted to a child's misbehavior.

Most people will agree that when they were children, they were not allowed to get away with many of the things children of today expect as their birthright. Today, children are generally more comfortable expressing their emotions, and they also have different expectations of their parents. This shouldn't surprise us—just like we, as adults, have risen our expectations of our governments, employers, or service providers compared to the generation of our parents, so do children of today expect many things and privileges we were not entitled to while we were growing up.

The worst thing a parent can do when facing an angry child is to try to stop him or her from being angry. When you do that, as many parents do, you are forcing your child to suppress their emotions. If the consequence of throwing a tantrum is punishment, a child will quickly learn that anger is something that should not be displayed openly. But this doesn't mean they will stop feeling angry, only that they will stop expressing their emotions for fear of punishment.

Not surprisingly, such children usually grow up into adults who rarely show their feelings. This, in turn, creates many other problems, because bottled-up emotions will sooner or later have to find an outlet. This explains why otherwise perfectly normal, kind, and tolerant people physically or mentally abuse their families, or even get involved in violent crime.

So, rule number one: never try to suppress or ignore the fact that your child is angry, because there is probably a very good reason why he or she feels that way.

6 common reasons why children get angry:

1. **They can't get what they want**

    Children are more intelligent than we give them credit for, and they quickly learn what works and what doesn't. So, if a child is used to being allowed to eat sweets all the time, he or she will react negatively when that favor is withdrawn. Parents often use such favors as a disciplining tool, and if they use it correctly and the child understands that favors are not automatically granted but have to be earned, everything will be fine. However, if a child assumes it is entitled to something which one day becomes unavailable, it will "fight for its rights."

2. **They are teased by peers or adult**

Often, gentle teasing is okay and adults sometimes do it to get children to do something, like saying "I know you can't count to 10" so the child will count to 10 to prove them wrong. However, teasing that makes the child feel embarrassed or stupid can easily provoke angry tantrums.

3. **They react to criticism**

Parents can be extremely demanding, although they believe they do it with the child's best interest in mind. Pushing a child to do something and then criticizing him or her if they fail can make a child angry. However, some children are very spoiled and are not used to criticism—by throwing a tantrum, they are setting boundaries and showing their parents what they can and cannot say.

4. **They are disappointed**

   Parents often make promises they have no intention of keeping, just to get a child to do something or stop crying. For a child that has been expecting to be taken to the zoo or given a new toy, this may be a major blow. On the other hand, spoiled children often bully their parents by throwing tantrums until they get what they want.

5. **Disagreement**

   This happens sometimes when children are playing with other kids. Children pick up basic social skills during interaction with their peers, but if a child is not used to losing or sharing, being put in a situation where this is required can trigger an angry outburst.

6. **Rejection**

   Children, as well as adults with low self-esteem, react intensely to rejection. Being part of a herd is very important to a child, so the reaction to being, or just feeling, rejected by peers or parents may result in hitting, biting, crying, tantrums, or withdrawal.

The easiest way to cope with your child's anger is not to expose them to situations that make them angry. However, this is not always possible, nor would it be a wise thing to do in the long-term. Anger is a part of life, and the best thing you can do for your child is to teach them how to control it.

Some children cope better than others. If your child is prone to anger outbursts, it's best to identify what triggers such behavior and control their exposure to such stimuli, like too much TV, certain games, or the presence of certain children or adults.

If a child takes a long time to stop screaming and tends to become physical when angry, you could be dealing with anger overload. This is not a typical reaction to anger, but is a prolonged outburst where the child is simply inconsolable and unable to stop screaming, crying, or thrashing around.

Anger Management for Kids

To manage anger, you first have to understand what is behind emotional outbursts. Understanding triggers can help you find a solution. In the case of excessive or prolonged anger, you could be dealing with an anger-related disorder. While medication can reduce some of the symptoms of hyperactivity or anxiety, only therapy can provide long-lasting improvement and help keep anger in control.

<u>4 common causes of excessive anger outbursts:</u>

1. Hyperactivity
2. Anxiety
3. Trauma or neglect
4. Health disorders, like learning problems or autism

With young children, "normal" tantrums are common, especially if they feel frustrated or refuse to do something you're asking of them. This is often because very young children can't always explain what they want or how they feel, so they act it out. A tantrum is also the best way to draw attention to oneself, so children often use this as "sign" language to show they are not happy with something.

But sometimes, tantrums happen all the time. If they never seem to stop, or it becomes obvious that a child is unable to control his or her temper, this is usually a sign that you're dealing with a behavior problem.

<u>5 signs that angry outbursts could be a symptom of behavior problem:</u>

1. They don't stop even when the child is older than seven
2. The child's behavior becomes increasingly violent
3. They start getting into trouble at school
4. They can't get along with other kids, so they are often excluded from birthday parties or games.
5. Their behavior starts disrupting family life, like the relationship between parents or with other siblings.

As anger is often the only way a child knows how to react to frustration, parents should take angry outbursts seriously. Instead of telling the child to stop, they should try to figure out what made the child so upset. It is often the feeling of helplessness, quite common in children, that prompts them to express their feelings through anger.

Parents can do a lot to help their children learn how to cope with anger. First of all, they should encourage them to express their emotions, whatever they are, rather than deny them. Secondly, they should find a way of channeling those emotions into something positive. Finding an effective outlet for unexpressed feelings is one of the best ways of preventing them from becoming bottled up.

The reason some children seem to almost enjoy being angry is that an outburst is followed by an adrenaline rush, which boosts their energy. Suddenly, though temporarily, they feel <u>powerful</u> instead of <u>powerless.</u>

But if angry outbursts continue, maybe you as a parent need to reset your own boundaries, adopt a new set of rules, spend more time talking to your child, or take more interest in their life.

Whichever course your child's anger takes, make sure the child understands the difference between anger and aggression. To be angry is okay, being aggressive isn't.

Anger is often a cry for help, especially in very young children who may not be able to clearly explain what bothers them—but even they should be taught how to express their anger in the least harmful way. On the other hand, aggression, especially toward others, should not be tolerated, and this should be made very clear.

Anger Management

Talk to your child as often as you can and try to be aware of what is going on in his or her life, especially outside the home. Prompt them to tell you what is bothering them. To get to a stage where a child will open up, you have to develop a close and trusting relationship.

Don't forget that children copy the behavior of adults, and an excessively angry child may be responding to chaos at home, like alcohol, domestic violence, or abuse.

7 tips on how to deal with an angry child:

1. Praise your child often.
2. Criticize them if you have to.
3. Provide physical outlets.
4. Take an interest in your child's activities—ask about what happened at school, how they like their new teacher, how are their relationships with their peers.
5. Be a role model—if you don't want your child to use bad language or act aggressively, you shouldn't either.
6. Teach children that anger is normal, but that aggression isn't the answer
7. Don't get involved in any conversation as long as the child is screaming. Wait until they have calmed down to find out what has happened.
8. Don't give in to blackmail, but be prepared to listen.

Despite many new approaches to childhood education, discipline is and always will be the key to good behavior. It's about rules and rewards. It's about preventing behavioral problems, and teaching a child what behavior is and isn't acceptable.

As Nicole Ari Parker said, "Raising children is about loving them while trying to figure out how to discipline them."

Food for Thought:

1. Do you think children should get used to receiving criticism, or that they should be spared until they are at least 10 years old? Would too much criticism make them stronger or undermine their ego?

2. Considering their communication skills are limited, do you think children are justified in throwing tantrums? How else could they get adults to do what they want?

3. Think of a relative or a friend who has a child struggling with anger management. What are their parents doing about it? What would you do in their place?

Day 5

Anger in Teens

For a number of physiological, psychological, and social reasons, being a teen is the most difficult period of one's life. When your body is developing from that of a child to that of an adult and your hormones are wreaking havoc in your mind, it's not surprising that you often appear tense and angry.

A teen is but a child in an adult's body—faced with the physical and emotional needs of an adult, but neither fully developed physically and emotionally nor financially independent to be able to fulfill those needs. As a result, they, not surprisingly, often lash out in anger at those they feel are responsible for their unfulfilled needs – their parents.

Why are Teens Angry?

We've all been teenagers before, so we all know how hard growing up can be. In the past, and in some cultures even today, teenagers were more considered to be children than adults. Today, teenagers are—perhaps unfairly—often expected to behave and be responsible for things that normally only adults should deal with.

Handling a child who throws a tantrum can be hard, but it's nothing compared to dealing with an angry and screaming teenager who may be considerably taller and stronger than you.

Teens can be angry with or without reason, and it is up to their parents to curb or fuel that anger. Instead of yelling and fighting back, which may be very tempting but which would only escalate the argument, a parent should try to calm them down.

If you respond to your teen's anger by yelling or threatening, you put yourself on the same level as your child. In some ways, you become equal, which means you lose some of the "weight" at the bargaining table. If this happens, it may be even more difficult to negotiate further. So, whatever you do, don't lose control.

To deal with teen anger, you have to understand what makes them angry. As a parent, you know that although they may try to act like adults, the brains of adolescents are still developing. The way a teen perceives and experiences the world is very different from how an adult sees it, and this should not be used against them.

The problem with angry teens is not that they are often angry for no particular reason, but that they may not be expressing that anger effectively, either because they don't know how to or because they are not allowed to. Unaddressed anger makes people feel powerless and helpless and can sometimes lead to depression or violence—often turned against those who have nothing to do with their feeling of helplessness, but who happen to be an easy target, like pets, siblings, or friends.

The root cause of a teen's anger is usually due to physiological and emotional changes going on in their bodies, as they try to make sense of it. Their social background, as well as the support they get from their families, can either make this process easier or more difficult.

<u>4 things to do when facing an angry teen:</u>

1. Don't use bad language or name-calling, as this will only make things worse.

2. Never make any major decisions, promises, or threats, if you are both in a state. Wait for things to calm down, first. In fact, if both you and your teen are very angry, it's best not to say much. When you have both cooled off, you can address the problem in a more constructive way.

3. Never get physical, because this may easily escalate into violence.

4. Try to listen carefully to what they are saying—their comments or demands may be justified. Even if you don't do anything about it, show you respect them enough to listen to what they have to say. Teenagers

often feel ignored or belittled, and this can be a major anger trigger.

Adolescents are often moody and have strong feelings, which means they often can't think straight nor listen to reason. You shouldn't hold this against them—all the physiological and emotional changes they are going through makes them feel confused and angry.

A teenager's anger is usually directed at those they identify as an obstacle to their desires, which is usually their parents. Other times, they may not be angry with you, but because of something that happened at school or because of an argument with a friend.

Teen Anger Management

Although anger is not bad *per se*, to be used positively, it needs to be managed. There are different ways of expressing anger, and the trick is to express it effectively without hurting others, verbally or physically, or creating an atmosphere of discomfort and fear.

Teens may often seem angry, but are not always sure what or who they are angry with. As a result, they may be prone to snapping or sulking.

However, if a teen stays in this angry mode for months on end, without any particular reason, it could be a sign that their anger had turned inward. Those who sulk for extended periods of time may easily sink into depression, or become violent and start bullying others.

Angry teens can often become rude, asking for trouble, and behaving as if they want to turn every situation into an argument. With such individuals, discussing anything calmly is impossible, and almost any conversation easily spins out of control.

If such behavior becomes frequent, it could be a symptom of an anger-based disorder. Unfortunately, these disorders are particularly common with adolescents who were subjected to physical or mental abuse, or who through TV and video games are often exposed to images of violence, or those who were punished for being angry. Teens who received little or no support while growing up are much more likely to develop some kind of anger-based disorder later in life, simply because they never learned nor were allowed to express their emotions properly.

So, how do you deal with an angry teen? Assuming you understand where their anger is coming from, you will help them the most if you create an environment where they feel safe to express their feelings, regardless of what they are.

Another important thing to do is to try and establish a close relationship with your teen and encourage them to talk to you, so you are more aware of the people they socialize with. The older the teen, the more likely their behavior and values will be influenced by their peers, and peer pressure can lead to inappropriate and destructive behaviors.

10 ways to help teenagers handle their anger:

1. Become a role model on how to manage one's emotions.
2. Allow them to express anger.
3. Never punish them by humiliating them.
4. Be aware of who, outside of the home, may be influencing their behavior.
5. Set rules, but don't forget rewards.
6. Be open to negotiations, but say no to threats, blackmails, and tantrums.
7. Encourage intimacy and bonding, so you know what's going on in their life.
8. Never be too busy to listen to them.
9. Allow them to be open about their feelings.
10. Cultivate mutual trust and respect.

Food for Thought:

1. What were you like as a teen? Were you often angry? If yes, how did you deal with it?
2. When confronted by an angry person, what is the one thing you should never do?
3. When reasoning with an angry teenager doesn't work, how far do you think a teacher or a parent should go

with enforcing discipline? What do you think happens if parents hold different views on how to address their angry teen?

Day 6

Anger as Part of Grief

Just like you can be quietly or ecstatically happy, you can handle your grief with silent sadness or with a massive show of pain and outrage. Regardless of the way you choose to grieve for something or someone (like a way of life or a loved one), anger will definitely play a part in the process.

Why You Should Neither Ignore, Nor Feed Your Anger

There is a legend that one evening. an elderly Cherokee told his grandson about a battle that happens inside every one of us. The battle is between two wolves. One is Evil. It is anger, jealousy, envy, sorrow, regret, greed, arrogance, guilt, resentment, inferiority, self-pity, lies, false pride, superiority, and ego. The other is Good. It is love, joy, peace, hope, serenity, humility, kindness, benevolence, generosity, empathy, truth, compassion, and faith. His grandson thought about this for a short moment, then asked his grandfather, "Which wolf wins?" To this, his grandfather simply replied, "The one you feed."

Emotions are there to be experienced, not bottled up. However, if you experience negative emotions too often or you stay with them for too long, they can eventually become your reality.

Anger, being a very powerful emotion, should not be ignored—it is actually trying to tell you something. Nor should it be fed and nurtured, until it grows beyond control.

Grief is a very personal thing; there is no one-size-fits-all way to grieve. The way you go about it depends on many things, including your support system, your relationship with the deceased, your religion or culture, and your own coping skills. It takes time to get over the loss of a loved one, and although everyone may encourage you to move on with your life, you shouldn't rush through the process—allow it to unfold naturally.

If the crushing sadness makes you feel like you won't be able to go on, or your burning anger at those who could have prevented the death but didn't makes you scream for justice, grief can be frightening. And this is why many people who go through a grieving process end up alone, at the time when they need support the most.

What happens when you ignore anger during grief:

Ignored or unaddressed emotions often come to haunt us later in life. However, Western culture doesn't encourage people to experience overwhelming emotions. Instead, people are encouraged to block or alter them with drugs, divert their attention from what is happening to them with the hypnotic repetition of positive mantras, or simply engage in various feel-good activities.

It's believed that one of the reasons anxiety and depression are increasingly common is that many of our basic feelings are not expressed, but controlled by keeping them swept under the carpet.

If you're dealing with negative emotions, you should try to understand where they're coming from and try to release them. Negative emotions shouldn't be ignored, but nor should you become stuck in them for the rest of your life.

<u>What happens when you feed your anger while grieving:</u>

If, after a personal loss, you dwell on the injustice of it all and cry for revenge, what you are doing is feeding your anger. According to the Law of Attraction, you get more of what you focus on—so by focusing on anger, you attract even more anger and bitterness into your life.

Instead of feeding it, you should starve it and release it.

No matter how frustrated or let down you may feel because of your loss, the faster you stop wallowing in guilt or sorrow, the faster you can get on with your life.

As Ralph Waldo Emerson so wisely pointed out, "A person is what he or she thinks about all day long."

Anger Management

How Anger Helps You Deal with Grief

Anger is often, but not always, part of grief—it's best to think about it as a state in which most of us temporarily find ourselves. Grief can bring feelings of helplessness, regret, blame, or self-blame, and all these emotions can make you very angry. When you hurt, you often try to find someone to blame, which means grieving people often lash out at others.

However, the energy of anger is sometimes directed inward. Some people can start to blame themselves for what happened, or hate themselves for not having been able to do something to prevent the death of their loved one.

10 common recipients of misdirected anger in case of grief:

1. Yourself, for not having done more to prevent the death
2. The person who died, for having abandoned you
3. Surviving family members, or passengers, for not having died instead
4. Doctors, for not having done more to prevent the death
5. Destiny, for leaving you alone, ridden with debt, powerless, or helpless
6. God, for allowing a good person to die
7. Life, for being so unfair

8. The rest of the world, because life goes on as if nothing happened
9. Others, who have not lost what you've lost
10. Everyone who is happy

In that context, being angry is a way of channeling your grieving energy while you try to make sense of your loss. Anger is also usually followed by an adrenaline rush, which boosts your energy levels, giving you the strength to go on.

So, although anger can be painful and frightening, it also represents personal power—which means that it may prompt you to do something to change the situation you are in. And change means action. If anger is expressed positively, it can be channeled into activism, a process that helps release the pain and the feeling of helplessness.

If, on the other hand, you try to suppress your anger—pretending that "that's how it was meant to be," or "it was God's will," or "there was nothing we could have done," while seething with rage and holding onto your anger—the bottled-up emotions may find an outlet in the form of depression or be misdirected to others, like family or friends.

The best way to cope with anger during a grieving process is by acknowledging your pain, your loss, your fears, your despair, and whatever else you may be feeling.

Anger Management

5 ways to cope with anger during grief:

1. Try to understand how you feel about your loss. Stay with the feeling, even if it hurts.
2. If you feel very angry, try to work out who are you angry with and why.
3. Think of ways to rid yourself of anger in a non-destructive way, like through physical exercise, volunteering, writing, or reaching out.
4. If you can't cope with anger because the person who caused your loss got away with it, confront the person you hold responsible for what happened if that's an option you can take, but don't try to escalate the situation.
5. Seek professional help if you find it hard to go on.

Finally, to be able to grieve and deal with the anger that often accompanies it, you have to understand the six stages of grief that you'll be going through.

6 stages of grief:

- **Shock**

    This is how your mind tries to protect you from overwhelming pain: "What? No, it can't be!"

- **Denial**

    This is how your mind tries to protect you from reality: "No, it can't be true."

- **Anger**

    This is when you start grieving in earnest when the truth finally hits you: "Why? Why me?"

- **Guilt**

    You will sooner or later start lamenting why you hadn't done more to prevent your loss: "If only I'd been there, maybe he'd still be alive."

- **Pain and sorrow**

    This is the hardest and most frightening part of the grieving process, because by then, you are fully aware of what has happened and you are forced to face reality.

- **Release and resolution**

    This is the stage of grief where you start accepting the reality and getting ready to let go of the relationship.

However, having gone through all six stages does not mean you're over your grief. It will continue to come back and haunt you from time to time—to prevent this from happening, it's very important to deal with the pain and close this chapter of your life.

To heal, it's important to go through all the stages of grieving. Then, you can accept the reality, forgive yourself and others, and move on.

Food for Thought:

1. Think of a painful memory you can't get out of your head. Do you realize that by thinking about it continually, you are feeding your anger? What would it take to release it? Why would anyone enjoy wallowing in self-pity?

2. Think of a time when you lost someone. How did you deal with the loss? What was the prevailing emotion—anger or sadness?

3. When a loved one has a life-threatening disease, it gives everyone time to prepare for their departure. On the other hand, when someone dies in a car accident, it comes as a major shock. Which scenario causes more anger?

Day 7

How Anger Affects Relationships

Chronic anger has a devastating effect on relationships—not only because it destroys love and trust, but because it creates a toxic and often unsafe atmosphere at home. Just like gathering clouds can warn us of an approaching storm, chronic anger issues are often a sign of an accident waiting to happen.

Anger as a Medley of Emotions

Anger is a complex emotion and unless it is managed, can be devastating to your health, relationships, and career. If you have an anger problem, it's important to work on it when you are NOT feeling angry, instead of waiting for an angry reaction to try and find the best ways to deal with it.

However, anger doesn't appear out of the blue—it is a response to another emotion or particular triggers.

Just like happiness is contagious, so is anger. When you are angry, it spills over to your environment, even if you aren't making a scene. Those around you can pick up on your quiet anger and, depending on their relationship with you, may feel intimidated or simply uncomfortable in your company. As a result, they may start avoiding you.

Although people in your environment—be it your family, colleagues, or friends—may have nothing to do with the reason you're angry, they often find themselves the target of your anger. You may snap at them, be sarcastic, or openly lash out. And this is what ruins many relationships.

When you start taking your anger out on others, especially if they are in no position to respond or physically remove themselves from you, your anger becomes a sort of bullying. If you know this is happening, the first thing you need to do is acknowledge that you have an anger problem which is getting out of control.

The best way to deal with a chronic anger issue in a relationship is to address the real cause; however, how you approach this will depend on who is having the problem.

If YOU have an anger problem:

- Look for a solution to this problem cool-headed. In other words, calm down first so you can think clearly. Anger releases certain hormones in our brain which can affect the decision-making process.
- Acknowledge your uncontrolled anger is creating problems in the relationship.
- Dig deep and try to understand why you feel so angry. It may have nothing to do with your partner, so why are you taking it out on them?

- Discuss your anger with your partner. Ask them how they feel during your outbursts. Try to see yourself through your partner's eyes and understand how this has been affecting your relationship.

- Together, make a plan for how you can start managing your anger. If nothing else, promise yourself you will refrain communicating with your partner or making any major decisions when overwhelmed with frustration, fear, or rage. Chances are, you will say or do things you'll regret later.

If YOUR PARTNER has an anger problem:

- Help him or her calm down when they are in a state.
- Listen to what they have to say, even if you don't agree with them. Let them speak. Even when people have every reason to feel angry, they will often vent their anger while talking about it, so confrontation is avoided.
- Communication is key for healthy relationships—the more you talk to each other, the less likely you are to have communication problems.

If BOTH PARTNERS have an anger problem:

- Dealing with an angry partner is bad enough, but if both suffer from chronic anger problems, the relationship usually would not work. Especially if neither is used to apologizing, staying calm during an argument, listening, or accepting another's point of view.

Psychologists believe that the main problem with anger is what we do with it—do we manage it, do we ignore it, do we direct it toward others or toward ourselves?

Unfortunately, uncontrolled anger often leads to fighting, blaming, name-calling, or bringing up the past. The more of these things you do to your partner when you're angry, the more difficult it becomes to go back to normal once you've calmed down, for some words or actions cannot be taken back.

We know that anger often goes hand in hand with other emotions, like feeling ashamed, hurt, or frightened. According to psychologists, anger is like an iceberg—only 10% of it shows while the remaining 90%, which is unseen, is what really is making you angry. So, while to others you may appear angry, what you are actually feeling is fear, shame, hurt, and more. Find out what your submerged iceberg is made out of.

During an argument, an angry person will often criticize their partner, which is counterproductive.

<u>Here are 5 signs you're dealing with anger in your relationship the wrong way:</u>

- If you are criticizing the character, rather than the behavior of your partner.

- If the criticism is supposed to make them feel guilty.

- If you are not doing this to improve your relationship, but just trying to let go of your bottled-up tension—criticizing them just to make yourself feel better, regardless of how the criticism is making your partner feel.

- If you refuse to listen to what your partner has to say in their defense, but expect them to do as you say.

- If your criticism is insulting or belittling.

Misplaced Anger

hile anger is important, because it often tells us in no uncertain terms that something needs to change, it can also be a destructive emotion.

We live in a stressful and often very unfair world, and not everyone copes well with pressure. When dealing with everything they have on their plate proves too much, some people simply lose it.

Unfortunately, those who find themselves at the receiving end of their angry outbursts are usually not those who caused it, but those they have access to. In most cases, this is a family member.

While one way of managing anger is to make sure you find a positive outlet for your emotions, misplaced anger will easily destroy a relationship, especially if it happens repeatedly.

5 causes of misplaced anger

1. **Suppressed anger**

    As many a wife will testify, women often find themselves on the receiving end of their frustrated husband's emotions. Although talking to your spouse is a great way to relieve tension and frustration, it has to be done in a way that is not harmful. In other words, you shouldn't destress by stressing someone else out.

2. **Desperation**

    Regardless of what it is you feel hopeless about, depending on your nature, you may sink into depression, make scenes, or lash out in indignation.

3. **Not taking time-off**

    The more stress in your life you have to cope with, be it at work or at home, the more you need to take care of your mental health. If you can't afford vacations, at least take weekends off from time to time. The best way to unwind is to get involved in something that makes you happy—that's what hobbies are for.

4. **Negative mindset**

   Some people find it very difficult to see anything positive in any situation. Instead, they dwell on problems (both real and imaginary), wants, lacks, or potential disasters (theirs or global). Not only will this attitude make you feel miserable all the time, it will probably also make you very angry.

5. **Resentment**

   We all feel resentful from time to time, but if this emotion lasts for very long, it can become part of your character. This usually has to do with some injustice done to you, but instead of addressing it, some people choose to wallow in pain and bitterness for the rest of their lives.

The worst thing is that many people are fully aware that their anger is misplaced, but can't or won't do anything about it. For how long your partner will be able to put up with it depends on many things, but even if you are not aggressive when you're angry, misplaced anger is very toxic for a relationship.

5 reasons misplaced anger destroys a relationship:

- It creates a negative atmosphere at home.
- Angry outbursts are unpleasant, disrespectful, and unsettling.

- It's very belittling to be treated like a doormat.
- Chronically angry individuals are difficult to live with because you never know when the next outburst is coming.
- Such people may not be safe to live with, especially if they have a history of aggression.

Food for Thought:

1. What do you do when you feel your partner or friend is angry about something? Do you try to distract them from what's bothering them, or do you get them to talk about it?

2. Some people go for a drink after work so they can relax and diffuse their accumulated tension in order not to pass it on to their family. Others expect their partners to help them unwind, although it usually means they will have to listen to the well-known complaints, objections, or dramas. Which approach do you think is better?

3. If you often have to suppress your anger, how do you make sure it doesn't become bottled up?

Day 8

Anger in the Workplace

Although there are many reasons to get angry, in a private situation—with family or friends—you can say things or even behave in an inappropriate way and still be forgiven. In the workplace, however, the situation is very different. While you and your sibling or spouse may fight regularly and still love each other, if you scream at your colleagues, call them names, or shame them, you are likely to get fired. Most people know this and try to control their temper at work as much as they can, but, this can lead to the most common cause of anger in the workplace—frustration.

Why is the Workplace Anger so Common?

Frustration is the main cause of anger in the workplace. However, what lies behind this frustration is often that these people know that, for one reason or another, they have to remain in the job (or organization) they do not enjoy. This creates resentment, which is a form of long-lasting unresolved anger.

6 reasons people feel frustrated in the workplace:

Anger Management

1. Being passed over for promotion.
2. Having to do what you are told even if you know it won't work.
3. Having to report to a much younger or less intelligent person.
4. Having to report to women (in some cultures, this would be a major blow to many men).
5. Having to work after hours or on weekends with no pay (this is common in organizations planning for layoffs, where many people try to make themselves irreplaceable by showing they are willing to work extra hours for no pay).
6. Having to take the blame for your boss' wrong decisions.

Most employers would rather not employ frustrated employees—they are rarely motivated enough to achieve good results, and can be a potential threat to the organization if they start lobbying against the management.

For you, however, long-held frustration can be a major threat to your health. If unaddressed, the simmering bitterness can lead to burnout, heart disease, high blood pressure, stroke, depression, or other conditions.

And the more you feel you are stuck in your position, the more frustrated you'll feel. If, due to your age or lack of skills, you know you are unlikely to find a better job and know you have to stay with the one you're currently in, or if there are not many jobs available where you live, or if the pay is good, you may feel trapped in a job you hate or with people you have no respect for.

The causes of frustration in the workplace are too numerous to list, but they usually revolve around some kind of a disappointment, like a poor performance evaluation, unfair treatment, being micromanaged, or being criticized too often.

However, disappointment may also be caused by unrealistic expectations. Maybe you assumed you'd be promoted in two years, or that you'd be given a car to go with the job.

The reason you appear angry at work may also have nothing to do with the workplace. If you have a troubled or chaotic personal life, it is likely to affect your professional life, as well—the frustration one brings from home is often directed at one's colleagues. This is a typical example of misplaced anger of browbeaten wives and husbands.

Whatever the cause of your anger in the workplace might be, you have to try and manage it as best you can. Mild irritation is what we all learn to deal with, however, if something happened that made you see red and you feel you're about to make a scene—stop.

8 things to do if you get very angry at work:

1. Take a deep breath or several deep breaths

2. Slowly count to ten

3. Tell yourself to stay calm

4. Try to prevent tension in your muscles, jaw, head, or stomach. Keep breathing and try to loosen your muscles.

5. Walk away from your desk

6. Get out of your office or the building

7. Take a short walk, call a friend, or chat to a colleague you can trust

8. When you have calmed down, think through how to address the problem that made you so mad

How to Deal with Work-Related Anger if You're a Manager

An organization where anger seems to be present all the time is not a nice place to work in. It could be a major HR issue that's making staff unhappy, or just one or two people who, for their own reasons, enjoy stirring things up.

Try to find out who or what is behind this underlying anger. Consider the office safety regulations first, to make sure personal safety is not what's making employees lack focus or drive.

Some problems you may be able to deal with on your own, but in case of major issues, it's best to get professional help, lest things get out of control. Hiring an external consultant to talk to staff often helps, for they may feel less intimidated approaching someone outside of the company.

There may be situations when you have to make unpopular decisions, like redundancies, pay cuts, benefits withdrawal, and so on; however, a negative atmosphere in a company is usually a result of the prevailing culture. Although problematic individuals have to be dealt with, keep in mind that overall dissatisfaction easily turns into anger.

If anger prevails and you can't figure out what may be the cause, perhaps you need to look at this problem from different angles. If it turns out that certain individuals are causing trouble and raising tension (or expectations), it could be that stress from their private lives is spilling over to their work environment. While there is usually not much you can do about their personal problems, you can at least talk to them to see if there is anything you can do to help make things easier at work.

Anger is the workplace can be very difficult to deal with, and many managers turn a blind eye or postpone taking any action for as long as they can. As a manager, though, you must be mentally and emotionally prepared to take action, taking care not to overreact or underreact.

10 things a manager can do to help employees deal with anger in the workplace:

Anger Management

1. Create a professional workplace culture of tolerance and mutual respect.
2. Set rules and expectations and make sure all new employees are aware of them.
3. Encourage communication and, if possible, organize communication training for staff on a regular basis.
4. Be approachable.
5. Provide anger management training, which would show people how to deal with their anger and how to respond to angry colleagues.
6. Deal with inappropriate behavior as soon as possible. The longer you put off an unpleasant confrontation, the more likely it is to get out of hand.
7. Employees with anger issues can create an unhealthy atmosphere in the company they work for, so recommend anger management treatment or fire them.
8. Keep written records of such incidents.
9. Have a zero-tolerance policy in the case of aggressive behavior.
10. In case of major problems, always consult an attorney or an HR professional.

Food for Thought:

1. What do you find most frustrating in your workplace? Is that something beyond your control, or can you do something about it?

2. Were you ever in a situation at work where you took part in an argument you now feel embarrassed about? What happened to make you react like that? How would you deal in the same situation today?

3. If you were a manager and had to fire your best employee for sexual harassment to protect a temp who only started working two months ago, what would you do?

Day 9

Anger-Related Disorders

You may have an anger problem because of a health disorder you are struggling with, or you can develop a health disorder because of a long-standing unaddressed anger problem. In the modern world, anger-related health issues are becoming very common. It seems that as the world gets faster, the people get angrier. Anger can often lead to other negative emotions, like resentment, hatred, self-pity, fear, or aggression, and over time, these self-destructive feelings can turn into disease or illness.

How Anger Affects Your Health

People with chronic anger problems are often those who remain stuck in an injustice (real or imaginary) that has befallen them. There may be a very good reason why someone is angry, but for this emotion to be constructive rather than destructive, it has to be managed.

Unfortunately, many people accept injustice as part of their fate or karma, and live their entire lives feeling angry and bitter. Others, because they can't accept the situation but don't know how to deal with it, become irritable and aggressive. There are also those who are simply short-tempered, and their anger can be triggered by almost anything.

Although many situations are beyond your control, what you do have control over is the way you react. Unless you exert this control, the uncontrolled angry episodes can sap your energy and health very quickly.

We know being angry is not healthy, but it was only relatively recently that the World Health Organization recognized 32 disorders as directly linked to dysfunctional anger, the best-known ones of which are:

- **Intermittent Explosive Disorder**

    Individuals with this disorder display "the degree of aggressiveness which is grossly out of proportion to any provocation or precipitating psychosocial stressor." This disorder is believed to be behind most mass shootings. The strange thing is that most of these individuals don't have a prior history of aggressive behavior. Typically, they are normal, polite, and friendly people. Then, all of a sudden, a rejection or a stressful event pushes them to a breaking point, and they go on a rampage. Their action is supposed to "restore honor or repay the injury."

- **Oppositional Defiant Disorder**

    This disorder manifests as defiance and anger against authority, and is most common in children and adolescents. However, this is not a case of occasional frustration or disobedience. These individuals have frequent tantrums, refuse to comply, argue excessively, blame others for their mistakes, behave rebelliously, and are often vindictive.

What makes the diagnosis of anger-related disorders particularly difficult is that they often appear alongside another emotional problem. This means that if you see a therapist to seek treatment for anger, the real reason for your emotional dysfunction may be another disorder you are probably not even aware of, and it's this that makes diagnosis and treatment difficult.

Anger affects various processes in your body—digestion, assimilation, cell production, circulation, healing, immune system, and more. As a result, if anger persists for months or years, it's very likely to weaken your immune system and to directly or indirectly lead to a number of problems:

- Headaches
- Digestion problems
- Insomnia
- Anxiety
- Depression
- High blood pressure
- Heart attack
- Stroke
- Skin problems

The Most Common Anger Disorders

Anger becomes disordered if the individual exhibits pathological aggressive, violent, or self-destructive behaviors which are driven by chronically repressed anger. Fortunately, most of us figure out how to manage our anger, so anger disorders are likely to happen only to those whose anger was not only not managed, but was repressed for a long time.

Another cause of anger disorder is neurological dysfunction and substance abuse, which both affect the way we control our violent impulses.

<u>6 most common forms anger can take:</u>

1. **Chronic anger**

    This is anger which has lasted for a long time. It usually has a major effect on our immune system and may be the cause of other mental disorders.

2. **Passive anger**

    This type of anger is difficult to identify, because it does not have typical anger symptoms.

3. **Overwhelmed anger**

    This kind of anger happens if there is too much going on in your life, and you can neither do something about it nor can you cope anymore. In other words, this happens when you feel overwhelmed with life.

4. **Self-inflicted anger**

   This type of anger is usually the result of feelings of guilt, shame, or self-blame. It is directed inward and can be very self-destructive.

5. **Judgmental anger**

   This type of anger is common in people who are resentful about a situation or life in general.

6. **Volatile anger**

   With this type of anger, individuals find it hard to control themselves and often display aggressive behavior.

Anger management techniques can help you keep many of the anger-related health disorders under control, and studying anger management materials such as this one can help you understand what you're dealing with.

8 ways anger management helps you deal with your anger:

1. Teaches you about anger and how to use it positively
2. Helps you understand your anger and identify your anger triggers
3. Suggests ways of reacting in such situations
4. Shows you how to relax and defuse anger

5. Helps you identify thoughts and beliefs associated with anger
6. Shows you why dwelling on past problems or hurts is counterproductive
7. Helps you resolve conflicts
8. Helps you identify alternatives to revenge

Food for Thought:

1. Do you know someone with a health disorder? How do you feel in their company? How do you think they feel in yours?
2. Discuss three situations where having anger management skills would help you resolve conflict more professionally.

Day 10

Anger Across Cultures

How you react to anger depends on many things, including your age, gender, and circumstances. However, the definition of anger, and especially of what justifies angry behavior, is largely based on the culture one comes from. In some cultures, expressing your emotions—particularly anger—may be considered very ill-mannered, other cultures encourage people to openly demonstrate how they feel about something. So, while many may consider people from the East as stony-faced and emotionless, to Asians, Westerners probably seem very rude.

Cultural Norms and Emotions

Anger has many definitions, causes, and possible outlets. It is often associated with hurt feelings, frustration, and a desire for justice or revenge. However, as cultures hold different attitudes toward anger, local norms will either encourage or curb angry displays in public.

Comparative studies on the way children are brought up show that in China (as well as throughout the Far East) demonstrating emotions is curbed in children from an early age. Tantrums are usually ignored, and children are left to cry until they have calmed down. Considering their cultural values, this is necessary for a child to develop socially-acceptable behavior.

In many Eastern cultures— Chinese, Japanese, Thai—anger is something that is usually not discussed, especially not in public. Children are discouraged to mention it, e.g., complain about something, or are punished if they do.

In Western culture, however, parents usually fuss and fret over their children, particularly during their fits of anger.

Cultural norms also influence how much anger is considered normal for a man and how much for a woman. In most patriarchal societies, girls are raised not to show their emotions openly—particularly negative ones such as anger. Although things have changed a lot in the last 200 years, in the West, public display of anger is discouraged in girls even today.

On the other hand, boys were, in a way, expected to show a certain degree of assertiveness (often manifested as an angry or aggressive behavior). If they didn't, they were believed not to have the necessary confidence to succeed in life.

Still, in most cultures, boys' anger is tolerated much more than that of girls, even when it leads to aggressive behavior—anger is believed to be what distinguishes them from the feminine characteristics of being kind, quiet, and forgiving.

Display of Emotions in Public

Despite the fact that in the West, anger—especially if it leads to aggression—is discouraged and sanctioned, there is still a disproportionately high level of anger among children. Many believe that it is TV and Internet games behind most of the unhealthy behaviors.

But even very young children seem to show signs of anger and aggressiveness toward others, as we can see with school bullying. For this reason, in the West, everyone is encouraged to talk about their anger problems so they can be addressed and channeled on time—especially children.

Until relatively recently, social status played a major part in how much someone was allowed to express anger. In the West, it was generally believed that the lower classes exhibited more anger—likely because, due to their socio-economic condition, they had more reason to be angry.

In Japan, however, it was those of a higher social status who exhibited more anger, as a symbol of their authority. So, although the display of anger was generally considered very rude and was sanctioned, it was granted only to those who felt entitled to almost anything because of their social status.

While most American citizens don't refrain from expressing anger in public, including making a major scene if they're angry, people in the Far East tend to avoid conflict at all costs. Regardless of how they may really feel—angry, embarrassed, or sad—they will smile. However, this "happy face" is the result of lifelong social conditioning and does not mean they actually feel happy or relaxed.

Cultural norms dictate what is and what isn't allowed, and serve as a guide to socially-acceptable behavior. Western and Eastern cultures approach anger problems in completely different ways. In Western culture, people are encouraged to openly show positive emotions, and manage the display of negative ones, but they are still allowed to express them. In Eastern cultures, people opt for the "middle way" (i.e., Tao), constantly seeking a balance between positive and negative emotions.

They start instilling these values into their children as early as preschool, which means American and Asian children have different reactions to visual stimuli. While in Europe and America, children prefer exciting activities, cartoons, or comics, in the Far East, they prefer calm emotions—smiles instead of laughter, not overly competitive games, or not very excitable stories.

Additionally, while American parents will use every available opportunity to boost their children's confidence, Chinese parents are more likely to downplay their children's good results so as not to inflate their ego.

Finally, bestsellers in America contain much more excited and arousing content when compared to bestsellers in Asia. So, although many believe that we now live in a global village and that our cultures are merging into one, when you dig a little deeper, it becomes obvious that cultural differences are still very present, although often skillfully disguised.

PART 2

Anger Management

Day 11

When Anger Becomes a Problem

While expressing anger is okay, and is actually good for your health, if you do it inappropriately or start feeling it too intensely or too often, it stops being a normal emotion and becomes a problem.

During an angry outburst, your body produces certain hormones. If these are released too frequently or for too long, they negatively affect your health in a number of ways.

So, while releasing anger is an important part of your mental health, this only works if you do so in a way that does not jeopardize your physical health or alienate you from society.

The Primitive Brain

Anger often becomes a problem when your body and mind are not in alignment. Your reaction during a fight-flight-freeze situation is a remnant of atavistic behavior, which was important when we lived close to nature—and still is, for those who continue to live that way.

However, over the past 30,000 years, our bodies and our environment didn't change at the same rate. While our bodies and instincts remained the same as those of a caveman, our physical and social environments changed beyond recognition.

In the 21st century, we are no longer regularly exposed to dangers that would make the fight-flight-freeze instincts necessary for our survival. However, to survive the stress, constant change, and fast pace of the modern world, we now need a very different set of skills—and anger management is one of them.

Numerous studies on the importance of the brain in human development show that the so-called "primitive brain"—the part of the brain that concerns our survival instincts—is much more powerful and important than the part responsible for our cognitive abilities.

The studies show that regardless of how much control we try to exercise over the neocortex part of the brain—no matter how much we try to stick to morals, ethics, and good intentions—when we find ourselves in a life-threatening situation, the primitive part of our brain, the part dealing with instincts, takes over. This, according to neuroscience, explains why we so easily become overcome by rage or fear and are unable to stop it.

This means that although our bodies have remained, from an evolutionary perspective, similar to that of a caveman's, our minds "moved on" and continued to develop and adapt to the changed environment and circumstances.

For this reason, there is often a clash between what we think we should do and what we actually do. As our body's reaction didn't change in face of danger (not only physical danger), the saying "do what you feel is right" makes a lot of sense. However, although your body and your instincts may know what's best for you, you may not be able to act on it. Our world requires that we stick to laws, rules, and cultural norms which often go against our instincts.

Although the world has changed a lot, it doesn't mean we face fewer dangers today than we did all those years ago. The main difference is that the dangers of today don't come from our physical environment, like wild animals, hostile tribes, or starvation, but from our lifestyle.

<u>5 main "dangers" we face today:</u>
1. Chronic stress
2. Overpopulation and lack of personal space
3. Competitiveness
4. Fast living
5. The fast-changing world

As our physical bodies failed to change at the same rate with which our social environment has changed, our reactions to the stress and tension of the modern times is simply the result of our bodies trying to cope with the circumstances for which they were not designed. Therefore, the primitive parts of our brains react to these stressors the same way they would to an imminent attack by a wild animal or any other physical danger.

Unfortunately, not everyone copes well with stress. These stressors, especially if they happen too often or remain unaddressed, often make us angry.

As a species, we are faced with 4 major problems:

- Adapting to an environment that is changing much too fast
- Developing unhealthy lifestyles to match the changing environment
- Coping with stress
- Dealing with anger issues which often result from the stress the world seems to be drowning in

So, does this mean our primitive brain is why so many of us seem to be so angry all the time? Probably not. Our brains are simply trying to help us survive in the face of the threats we face, regardless of what they are. It does not distinguish between a hungry wolf about to attack and an angry boss who threatens to fire you. In both scenarios, you're in serious trouble, and the adrenaline rush is simply there to help you make the best decision under the circumstances and save your life or job.

However, we live in a sophisticated world and even if you are provoked and feel very angry, you should try to control your reactions.

Intense anger can lead to violence, which can result in physical injury, imprisonment, or even loss of life. Even if your anger does not lead to violence, if you express it inappropriately, your position in society may be seriously damaged. Violent and rude people can easily become social outcasts.

If you are known for your temper, others may feel intimidated in your presence and start avoiding you, refusing to have anything to do with your family, or preventing their children from socializing with yours. A poorly-managed temper may cost you your relationship, job, and health.

There are people who act angrily and aggressively not because they can't control their primitive brain, but because they feel good when they are intimidating others. Some may believe people are more likely to listen or respect them that way. Others may act aggressively because they never learned how to manage their anger and simply don't know a better way to express annoyance, resentment, or pain. When someone has been under significant pressure for a long time, they may no longer care how their angry outburst make others feel as long as they release the accumulated tension.

Another problem with anger is that it can become a habit. And as breaking a habit requires determination and perseverance, you may find it easier to stick to your routine rather than try to change it.

If you're struggling with anger, perhaps you should consider anger management counseling, where you can learn how to process it and release it in a way that is neither self-destructive nor harmful to your environment.

Can the Primitive Brain be Controlled?

Being unable to adapt to a changing environment is what's believed to have exterminated the dinosaurs. So, to avoid getting into trouble because of anger—yours or someone else's—you should learn to recognize the first physical signs of the emotion.

<u>7 early signs of anger:</u>
1. Tension in the shoulders
2. Headache
3. Foot tapping
4. Fast heart rate
5. Short breaths
6. Sweating
7. Facial flushing

What these physiological changes mean is that your body is telling you to get ready for action—maybe facing an angry client, being wrongfully accused of something you didn't do, or a possible animal attack.

It's crucial that at this stage you calm yourself down, before you say or do anything. The greater the danger, the more careful you have to be with how you'll react.

- Try to breathe more slowly and concentrate on your breath.
- Try to think what the best way is to resolve the issue.
- If the person facing you is angrier than you are, try to calm them down. Let them say what they have to say and try to get them to talk it over.

- It will help if you haven't used any alcohol or drugs prior to the incident, as both tend to lower inhibition and offer a false sense of power. Most angry and aggressive outbursts happen when alcohol is involved. So, if you're anticipating an unpleasant meeting, don't have a drink to brace yourself for the encounter. All you will achieve is a boost to your ego, which may cost you dearly.

- If you are not in imminent danger, when you've calmed down and hopefully lowered your blood pressure, try to talk yourself into a sensible solution. Alternatively, try to think about something positive.

However, this comes easier to some people than others. If you have a problem controlling your emotions and tend to overreact to provocations, injustices, or stress, it's time to consider anger management treatment.

So, although our instincts often help us get out of a sticky situation, we do need to adapt our behavior to the world we live in. If you know you have an anger problem, learning about anger management can help you understand where your emotions are coming from and how best to express them. However, there are some simple things you can do, starting from today, that will make you less prone to rash behavior or overreaction.

3 simple ways of taming your temper:

1. **Physical exercise**

    If you lead a very stressful life, or for some reason often find yourself in situations or with people who provoke an angry reaction in you, you should make physical exercise an essential part of your life, as it will help you release tension.

    Well-known psychologist V Schutt believes exercise helps dissolve anger because it helps you channel your emotions. Scientists are still not sure how this happens, but believe it has something to do with the way physical exercise affects the serotonin levels in the brain, which help regulate behavior. Physical exercise is particularly important for those who have aggressive tendencies.

2. **Mindfulness**

    If you are used to tuning in to your emotions, perhaps mindfulness can help you understand why you feel and react the way you do. When you feel angry, how does your body react—what happens in your chest, face, heart, stomach? How do you feel— exploited, helpless, abandoned—and why? What are the thoughts that go through your head?

    When you have calmed down, try to discuss the incident that made you angry with the person involved. Try not to start with accusations, but by explaining how the incident made you feel.

Being mindful about your anger is about admitting to yourself that you're not coping well, but also that you don't want to ignore your negative emotions—you want to do something about them. Anger management can be a difficult and long process, so be patient with yourself.

3. Meditation

Meditation is an easy and simple way of preventing anger from getting out of control. Although there are many different ways to meditate, all revolve around self-awareness.

The practice of meditation helps you recognize the signs of anger, so you can learn how to react when you notice anger building up.

In other words, meditation improves your self-control and ability to calm your mind by focusing on something positive. If you practice it daily, you will soon become calmer and less stressed out, which will indirectly change the way you react to anger-provoking situations.

Meditation has been successfully used to deal with problematic adolescents and even in the rehabilitation of violent criminals.

Day 12

Handling Emotions

There is a proverb that "a man without self-control is like a city broken into and left without walls."

Emotions, both positive and negative, are a normal part of our lives—provided they are kept under control. Emotions help us understand how we feel about something or someone, like whether we can relax or should be on our guard, whether we can count on someone or not, how self-confident we should feel under the circumstances, and so on.

Still, we shouldn't allow our feelings to rule our lives, but should aim to take charge of them and rule them, instead. And this only happens if you know how to handle your emotions.

How to Take Charge of Your Emotions

Most of us know, sometimes subconsciously, what sort of situations or individuals push our buttons. And, if we give it some thought, we can better prepare ourselves to face emotionally-charged situations or difficult people ahead of time.

Just like how you prepare for an important meeting or an interview, if you know that finding yourself around certain people or in a certain situation is likely to make you feel angry and act inappropriately, work on bracing yourself for the event.

You can do this by preparing yourself mentally and emotionally for what you think is likely to happen. That way, since you have a better idea of what to expect, you'll be ready to deal with those challenges in a positive and constructive manner.

When you take charge of your emotions, you can prevent the situation from getting out of hand. This is particularly important for situations which are likely to escalate and for those who know they have an anger problem.

So, assuming you find it hard to control your temper or often find yourself in situations which make you behave inappropriately, you should prepare an Action Plan for handling your emotions.

<u>8 things to do when you want to improve the way you handle your emotions:</u>

1. Avoid if you can

Whenever possible, try to avoid the situations and people that are likely to make you angry. Unfortunately, this is often not possible, and all you can do is hope to have enough time to prepare mentally and emotionally before confronting them.

2. Emotions are a matter of choice

With a healthy dose of self-control and emotional intelligence, it's easy to avoid getting angry—even in the company of those who easily push your buttons. Being able to handle your emotions is about taking full control of how you react to anger triggers.

3. Try to make the situation less tense

It's often possible to defuse the tension if you make a conscious effort to do so. For example, if you know that a friend is touchy about certain issues, avoid discussing them. If your boss is particular about punctuality, make an effort to get to work on time. We often do things we know irritate others either because we're too lazy to make an effort, because we enjoy pushing their buttons, or because we are so self-centered we simply don't think about how what we say may make others feel.

4. Ask yourself why certain individuals or situations trigger such an angry response in you

Sometimes, when you are angry with others, you may actually be angry with yourself. It's not uncommon to project what we feel about ourselves onto others. For example, if someone's arrogance makes you angry, are you sure it's not because you reserve arrogance for yourself and are annoyed that someone else is behaving the way you think YOU are entitled to act?

We often say to others what we should be saying to ourselves—"Don't be so impatient," "Why are you so selfish?" So, the saying "It takes one to know one" makes a lot of sense.

5. Try to ignore the triggers

If you know that in certain situations you always get angry, try to shift your focus. For example, if you find the way someone dresses irritating, try to shift the focus from their clothing style to other aspects of their personality, like their work ethics or their empathy. It's easy to get angry if you focus on what you don't like or disapprove of.

6. Change your thoughts

If you can control your thoughts and attitudes, you'll have no problem controlling your emotions—your thoughts create your emotions. When you stop focusing on the negative in your life, such as rude colleagues, unfair working conditions, family struggles, or the consequences of environmental pollution, you will automatically feel less angry. And if you get to a stage where you can feel genuinely happy for others, you will become less judgmental, more compassionate, and will rarely feel angry.

7. Change your reaction

Changing the way you react to a trigger is not easy—it's something you have to work on all your life. However, when you can control your emotions, you have control over your life. By making an effort to choose your response to a trigger, you are taking control of a potentially chaotic situation. It's well-known that anger breeds anger—when you choose to react angrily, be prepared to receive a similar reaction from others.

8. Focus on the solution, not the problem

Instead of constantly thinking about how horrible the people you work with are, try to either change them, change yourself, accept the situation, or find another job. By focusing on the negative in your life, like a disloyal friend, a dead-end relationship, a low-paying job, failing health, you are making yourself bitter and irritable. Wallowing in self-pity and anger can't bring you anything good, so why do it? Why not try to find a solution to your problem, instead of ruminating about the unfairness of life?

How to Control Angry Emotions

We can usually see an angry reaction coming, like when the meeting is not going in the right direction or when we know in advance that a particular situation is likely to turn nasty. This means we usually have time to prepare ourselves for situations which we suspect may provoke an angry reaction, either in us or in others.

If you want to be the master of your life and you know you have an anger problem, try to adopt practices which can help you control both the anger triggers and your reaction to those triggers.

<u>6 habits that can help you control your emotions in any situation:</u>

1. Tune into your inner self

This is a very useful exercise, particularly when you're feeling unhappy, upset, or angry. Start by asking yourself why you are feeling that way. Pay attention to any emotions or thoughts that come up—sadness, anxiety, envy, rage, and so on.

Tuning in is about being in touch with your innermost feelings. It's about reconnecting with your intuition. Most of us have been encouraged not to rely on our gut feelings, but to base our decisions on our logical minds.

Listening to your intuition in the noisy, neurotic, and stressful world can be difficult. Not only have most of our instincts become dormant, but we rarely trust them. Your intuition or gut feeling can be a source of wisdom and, often, your best guide. But to receive this guidance, you have to listen to it and learn to understand what it's trying to tell you. This starts when you tune in to your inner self.

Your inner voice is nothing more than your subconscious telling you what's best for you under the circumstances. However, it may not say what you'd like to hear, and that's often the main reason why you choose to ignore this voice.

2. Develop emotional intelligence

Emotionally intelligent people have great people skills. They are not only in touch with their feelings, but are able to tune in to the feelings of others.

Emotional intelligence enables people to understand themselves and learn where their feelings are coming from. As a result, their reactions are timely and appropriate. They are good at listening, which not only improves their communication skills, but prevents emotionally-charged situations from getting out of hand.

Basically, managing emotions is about working out what triggered a particular emotion and not responding until you've had time to process that emotion. The best thing is that when you can manage your emotions, you can easily manage any situation you find yourself in.

3. Develop a positive mindset

Being positive about life is good for your health, your relations, and your overall happiness.

In line with the saying that "like attracts like," staying positive even when things are not going well is the prerequisite for success. When you are positive about life, it's easy to feel good about yourself, and this makes it easier to deal with anger—both yours and other people's.

4. Mindfulness

Applying mindfulness techniques is very useful when you feel you're beginning to lose it or feel you need more balance in your life. First of all, recognize what's happening (I'm getting angry). Give yourself time to think about how to respond (Count to ten). Respond calmly (Suggest a short break, postpone the meeting for another time, or try to look at the problem from a different angle or in a way that would give both parties a chance to reconsider their position).

5. Identify your anger threshold

You have to know when to draw the line and remove yourself from a situation that is not going anywhere and is likely to get out of hand. Depending on the situation, you may suggest a different approach, consult with someone, or simply walk away. Sometimes, removing yourself from the scene is all it takes to defuse a tense moment. However, it's important you do this BEFORE things get out of hand.

6. Recharge before start running on empty

Negative emotions, such as anger, create negative energy which is not only self-destructive, but quickly depletes your vitality and enthusiasm. To fight back, find out what activities boost your mood and do them whenever you feel subconscious negativity creeping up (this could be taking your dog for a walk, sitting in the garden, meditating, chatting to someone, listening to uplifting music, and so on).

To quote Zen Buddhist monk Thich Nhat Hanh, "When you say something unkind, when you do something in retaliation, your anger increases. You make the other person suffer, and they try hard to say or do something back to make you suffer, and get relief from their suffering. That is how conflict escalates."

Day 13

Emotional Intelligence and Anger Management

When most people think of emotional intelligence, they seem to imagine it as a set of skills that can make them more employable. This is partly true—being a good team player, working easily under pressure, and being able to communicate effectively in a culturally-diverse environment increases your chances of getting hired.

However, these same skills are just as important outside work, and maybe even more so. Your ability to understand and manage your emotions and be able to process them before responding will impact how successfully you deal with challenges on both the personal and professional level.

Emotional intelligence is much more than empathy and good people skills. It's about self-awareness and self-management: the very skills you need if you're struggling with anger.

What's Emotional Intelligence and Why Is It Important

Emotional intelligence skills revolve around the ability to understand and manage your own emotions, as well as those of others. Managing emotions is about understanding what triggers them, but choosing not to respond to the trigger until you've had time to process the emotion. And when you can manage your emotions, you can manage any situation you may find yourself in.

The ability to manage your emotions can be of great help in many different situations, like with decision-making or conflict resolution, but particularly with avoiding situations which could lead to conflict.

For anyone who has contact with others (as most of us do), conflicts are an unavoidable part of life. They are not necessarily bad, because they sometimes help get issues and emotions out in the open. So, if you can control your emotions, you can take control of your life and relationships.

Relationship problems happen both inside and outside of work, and although you would use a different technique when resolving a diplomatic conflict than an argument with a friend, you still need to be emotionally intelligent to successfully address the situation.

Learning about emotional intelligence is not difficult, though it comes easier to some than to others. For people who are empathic by nature, these skills are a way of life, and they—often unknowingly—apply them to whatever they do. On the other hand, those who are not in touch with their own feelings, and who care even less for the feelings of others, have to make an effort to start thinking and behaving in an emotionally intelligent way.

Many people learn emotional intelligence on the job, like when they find themselves in situations that require tolerance, patience, and empathy. However, it's much better to acquire these skills before you find yourself in a delicate situation.

What distinguishes emotionally intelligent people from others is that they know themselves well, so they understand why they think and react the way they do. When you have a high level of self-awareness, you understand what's going on in your mind, even if you don't approve of it. And it's easier to deal with something you understand.

We all get angry from time to time, but an emotionally intelligent person will always try to process the emotion they are experiencing. This is important, since your anger is often just a reaction to something else, even something you may not even be aware of like the memory of an old hurt.

Emotional competency can truly change your life and enhance your chances of success on all levels. There are many techniques at your disposal if you want to master emotional intelligence skills, but to truly benefit from them, you have to apply them to everything you do.

Emotional intelligence is also about developing an awareness of how your behavior affects others—an emotionally intelligent person is fully aware of this, regardless of the situation they find themselves in.

<u>2 main benefits of emotional intelligence:</u>

- **You're in complete control of your emotions**

When you can control your emotions, you can control your life. And when you can do that, you can take a proactive role in how your life pans out.

- **You easily avoid or resolve conflicts**

    Although emotionally intelligent people are good at resolving conflicts, their main advantage over others is that they know how to prevent a situation from getting to a stage where it becomes an open conflict.

How Emotional Intelligence Helps with Anger Management

Emotional intelligence is mainly about self-awareness and self-management. People who are self-aware rarely allow themselves to get carried away, even when feeling angry, while self-management helps them control their angry thoughts and emotions.

So, if you are often overwhelmed with negative thoughts, which create negative emotions and result in angry outbursts, you need to address your anger problem as soon as possible.

However, if you believe that your behavior does not require therapy, you can try and modify it by improving your emotional intelligence skills. This is only possible if you practice self-awareness, which can be achieved when you start paying attention to and trying to understand your thoughts, emotions, and behavior.

<u>6 ways to develop emotional intelligence:</u>

1. **Self-Analysis**

    If you really know yourself, you will understand why you feel and react the way you do. When you understand the WHY (you react a certain way), it becomes easier to figure out the HOW (you should behave instead).

2. **Self-awareness**

    Learn how to tune in to your emotions, regardless of what they are, and try to understand how they affect your thoughts or decisions. Ask yourself why you feel the way you do.

3. **Understand where your anger is coming from**

    Negative feelings are easier to deal with if you name them. Even if you can't do anything about them at the moment, knowing what you're dealing with is part of the solution.

4. **Don't rush to respond to a trigger**

    Whenever you feel angry, give yourself time to think before responding. Depending on what you're responding to, you may consider putting off your response for later. If that's not possible, simply count to 10, or 50, or as long it takes so you don't say something you may later regret.

5. **Try to tune in to the emotions of others**

   Unfortunately, most people are neither good listeners nor do they have time to spare for others. Try approaching others with an open mind so you can "read" into the situation and get a feeling for how they feel.

6. **Be flexible**

   Accept that regardless of how strong your views on a particular topic might be, there may be situations where you have to be more diplomatic. Be prepared to adjust your words, actions, or reactions to the situation.

7. **Recognize and name**

   All emotions—especially negative ones—have to be recognized and named so you can address the REAL cause of your reaction.

8. **Emotional regulation**

   This is about learning how to control your strong emotions, particularly negative ones, and not acting on impulse. Practice by thinking of something that will make you feel hurt, angry, or exploited. Sit with the feeling—feel it, "digest" it—and after about five minutes, "respond" to the person or situation that made you feel that way.

You can't manage a situation (or a team, a relationship, etc.) unless you can manage yourself. We live under a lot of stress, which often makes otherwise peaceful people lash out in anger. Although shouting, slamming doors, or using strong language can help you release that pent-up anger, such behavior is unacceptable in public. The benefits of getting rid of your anger will be weakened by the fact that you'll later have to apologize to those who felt hurt or threatened by your behavior. And it may even cost you your job, or a relationship.

The key advantage of being emotionally intelligent is that you become more aware of how what you say and do affects those around you. It not only makes you a better leader, but also a better human being.

Day 14

Emotional Intelligence

In the overpopulated, dynamic, and fast-changing world, it's becoming difficult to cope—let alone succeed personally and professionally—without emotional intelligence skills. However, the dwindling job market, overcrowded workspaces, and increasing demands on our time all contribute to the stress and frustration we have to deal with almost on a daily basis.

Managing one's emotions is key to emotional intelligence, but this doesn't mean you have to feel positive about life regardless of what's going on around you.

Managing your emotions is about learning to react to fear, frustration, disappointment, or stress in a way that will reduce anxiety and tension in both yourself and others, rather than make an already tense situation worse.

Recognizing and Managing Your Emotions

Our emotions are the result of our thoughts, experiences, and mindset. And although it's not possible to change your past experiences, it is possible to change your thoughts and your attitude.

You may be feeding yourself negative thoughts, or you may be in a situation where you are fed such thoughts by those around you, such as your parents, partner, or friends.

Fortunately, thoughts can be changed and the power to change your thoughts and behavior lies with you.

It's unrealistic to expect anyone, no matter how emotionally intelligent they are, to always feel positive about life. Much of how we feel and think has to do with the people we come into contact with or the environments we live in. For example, in a war zone or a poverty-stricken neighborhood, it's difficult to be positive about anything, especially if you feel stuck. Many people feel just bad about themselves or their lives despite having everything they could wish for.

To manage emotions, you must never suppress them. This is why many therapists disapprove of mantras and positive affirmations. Instead of acknowledging you are sick, without an income, or in a messy relationship, by repeating a positive mantra—"I'll be fine", or "I am healthy and full of energy" or "I am confident the Universe will provide"—you are wasting time waiting for someone else to provide a solution to your problem.

Positive affirmations can be very helpful when you're feeling down, because it's definitely better to believe your circumstances will improve than it is to tell yourself you're in a hopeless situation. However, this only works as a temporary measure, until you find a creative solution to your problem. In other words, positive affirmations are simply a tool for boosting your self-confidence until you actually do something about the problem. The focus is on action.

There may be occasions when pushing your emotions out of your mind may help you deal with them. When powerful feelings stay bottled up for too long, especially if they concern a traumatic experience, they can affect your behavior, health, and mindset.

Managing emotions is not about repressing them, but addressing them in a positive and constructive way.

<u>3 tips on how to prevent negative emotions from becoming bottled up:</u>

1. **Talk about them**

    Emotions become bottled up because some experiences are not easy to talk about, you may not know how to express your feelings, or you may have no one to talk to. Some people may also think expressing emotions is a sign of weakness.

    An emotionally intelligent person knows that releasing emotions is an important part of mental health, necessary for your emotional and mental well-being.

    Unaddressed emotions eventually become emotional baggage, which some people carry around their whole life. Your emotional health depends on your memories and experiences, and the more traumas in your life, the greater the need to unpack that emotional baggage and let it go. On their own, old wounds may heal on the surface, but memories of shame, grief, guilt, or regret can create scars which, if unreleased, may stay with you forever.

2. **Write them down**

   If you can't talk about your emotions, try writing them down. That way, you can still get them out of your system without anyone learning about your secret. To make sure no one sees, destroy the written evidence once you've finished.

3. **Learn how to get rid of negative emotions**

   There are many ways to let go of anger, fear, sadness, jealousy, and other negative emotions. If these emotions are so overwhelming they are preventing you from leading a normal life, you should consider therapy. If they are less problematic, you can try self-help techniques, like physical exercise, journaling, self-therapy, meditation. Getting rid of negative emotions is particularly important if you have low self-esteem and a tendency to turn your anger inward.

However, try as you may, some types of anger may not be possible to get rid of. Either because the injustice done is unforgivable, like child abuse, or because you simply can't get over something, such as someone much less competent than you being promoted and becoming your boss.

However, although anger may be justified, holding on to it is not. If the damage cannot be undone, for your own peace of mind, you should try to resolve the negative effect of anger. This is crucial because as long as you're holding on to it, it will continue to harm you—without you even realizing it.

The Burden of Unresolved Anger

We often, unknowingly, hold on to anger by revisiting painful memories from the past which we can't or won't let go.

To let go of the anger, you first have to understand how self-destructive it can be and how it can cause many problems without you even realizing what's going on.

All emotions need an outlet. When anger is not released, it affects your body, which affects how your mind works, which in turn affects what sort of emotions you end up living with. Instead of letting repressed anger rule your life, take charge by letting go of everything that is no longer serving you, or that is undermining your health and well-being.

<u>4 steps to letting go of anger:</u>

Step 1: Are you aware of how anger is affecting your life?

To see the full impact of how anger is making you feel and behave, write down the answers to these questions.

1. How does anger make you feel?
2. How much time each day do you spend feeling angry?
3. Do you often wake up feeling angry?
4. Is anger often preventing you from falling asleep?
5. Do you indulge in comfort foods or alcohol when feeling angry? Does it help?
6. How does anger affect your performance at work?

7. How does anger affect your personal relationships?
8. What would it take for you to let go of this anger?

Step 2: Imagine your life without this bottled-up anger

Write down your answers.

1. If you didn't feel angry, how would you feel in the morning upon waking up?
2. If you didn't feel angry, would you drink less?
3. How would not feeling angry affect your relationships?
4. How would not feeling angry affect your performance at work?
5. How would you feel about your future if you didn't have this anger?

Step 3: Accept the things you cannot change

Have you identified the real cause of your anger? If you could turn back time, what would you do differently that would make it possible to live free of anger?

1. List three things you would change in your behavior.
2. What's stopping you from changing those behaviors now?

3. Can you accept your regrets as mistakes you can learn from?

Step 4: Acceptance

Think about your anger. Write down your answers.

1. Are you in any way responsible for the hurt that's making you angry?
2. Have you considered the possibility that the person who made you angry had no other option?
3. Have YOU ever done something similar to someone else?

Step four can be painful but is very powerful. Depending on the source of your anger, it may take you a long time to get to a stage where you can look at the problem from the other person's point of view.

It's believed that only once you take full responsibility for your anger, and understand your own role in it, can you truly get over it.

Day 15

Mindfulness

Mindfulness is about being fully focused on what's going on around you, what you're doing, what you're saying, and how you're feeling. Although this probably sounds simple enough, it's easier said than done—our minds are not easy to keep still.

Due to stress, information overload, or busy lifestyle, keeping your mind from wandering can be quite a challenge. The racing thoughts, the inner chatter, or things you unconsciously worry about all the time, can make your mind cluttered and restless.

The key to mindful living is the focus. A mindful person is totally in the moment, whether he's playing with his child, working, eating, making love, rock climbing, or writing a letter to a friend. He's aware of the effect his words or actions may have on others, so he thinks before he speaks or acts.

Mindfulness can be learned and it can also become a way of life; however, it does require an effort on your part to keep your mind focused on one thing amidst all the distractions that surround us. Many activities can help you cultivate this personal development technique, such as yoga, meditation, visualization, and sports.

How Mindful Are You?

Practicing mindfulness has many benefits for your health, happiness, work, and relationships. Both science and experience show all areas of your life improve once you start living mindfully.

However, being mindful in this day and age is not easy. Studies indicate most people spend nearly 50% of their waking hours thinking about something that has nothing to do with what they are doing, and this indirectly affects their performance, creativity, concentration, and well-being.

<u>13 things a MINDFUL person does:</u>

    1. They find it easy to focus on tasks.

    2. They make good use of their time.

    3. They get things done promptly.

    4. They are not easily distracted.

    5. They prioritize and stay focused on the most important things.

    6. They always find time to respond to emails, meet friends, and visit family.

    7. They are fully present during meetings.

    8. They find it easy to concentrate on what they're doing.

    9. They think before saying something.

10. They choose to "sleep on it" rather than make a hasty decision.

11. They stay calm under pressure.

12. They are fully aware of how they feel about someone or something.

13. They find it easy to understand how others feel.

<u>8 things THOSE WHO LACK mindfulness do:</u>

1. They are often surprised by what they say or do.

2. They often multitask.

3. They worry about work even after leaving office.

4. They often forget things other people say, things they read about, or promises they make.

5. They are uncomfortable sitting still or being quiet for long, and would rather be doing something.

6. Their mind wanders.

7. When they are upset, they can't stop thinking about it.

8. They often have trouble sleeping because their thoughts keep them awake.

Our scattered minds do the best they can to keep track of all the things we need to remember. However, in this stressful world, we wear so many hats in a single day that it's small wonder we are often highly-strung and anxious.

<u>3 simple mindfulness exercises that will force you to slow down and focus on something:</u>

1. Mindful observation

This exercise will help you notice, perhaps for the first time, how beautiful, unusual, or interesting some things you never thought about before are.

Choose an object from your immediate environment, like your garden, the park you walk your dog in, or something you keep on your balcony. It should be something that's been there for years, which you never bothered to notice before—a flower, a bird that visits your bird feeder, a piece of rock, a fallen tree trunk, a tree in full blossom.

Look at the object for as long as you can stay focused. Relax as you do so.

Examine its shape, color, and size, picking up even the tiniest details. As you do so, try to tune in to this object and imagine what its purpose in the web of life must be.

If you can get yourself to stay focused for 15 minutes without answering your phone or talking to someone, you'll be amazed at how refreshed you'll feel afterward.

2. Mindful immersion

This exercise is about finding contentment in what you do instead of moving continually from one activity to another. The purpose is to enjoy whatever it is you are doing at the moment.

For example, if you are involved in otherwise boring and repetitive work, such as doing housework, working in the garden, or sorting out files at work, try to approach these tasks from a different angle. Make your work more creative.

Pay attention to every single detail of your activity, as if you had to describe to someone how such a job should be done. Focus on what you are doing, and focus on how your body feels, how your muscles move as you lift or move things around.

By becoming aware of every step and immersing yourself in it, the job will be finished quickly. You'll stop thinking how boring it is and you'll stop pushing yourself to get it over with as soon as possible so you can move on to something else. You may even start enjoying it.

3. Mindful loving

When you are mindful in love, you don't wait for someone's birthday, anniversary, or Valentine's day to reflect on the importance of that relationship in your life. From time to time, stop and look back on the connection you have with a friend, spouse, or a parent. Reflect on all you've been through, appreciate that they are in your life, and show them you care. Don't just *think* about how much they mean to you—tell them how you feel.

Mindfulness and Anger Management

Cultivating mindfulness helps you reduce both the frequency and the level of the anger you experience.

Mindfulness is about being fully present in whatever you do. To some, this comes naturally, but most of us have to learn how to cultivate mindfulness. And one of the easiest ways to learn this is through meditation.

The practice of mindfulness meditation does not have to be complicated. You can do it while walking your dog, sitting quietly in the garden, listening to uplifting music, or as a part of other activities such as yoga, sports, or knitting. Simply put, mindfulness is about being "centered," without being aware of it. With practice, it becomes a way of life.

Mindfulness can make it easier to cope with life while improving your physical health by relieving stress, lowering blood pressure, and reducing chronic pain.

If your life decisions are made mindfully, it means you will have thought them through. For example, if you decide to go vegan, a mindful approach to this decision should be well thought-through and creative.

5 characteristics of mindful vegans:

- They understand and accept the challenges that a new way of life brings.
- They are prepared to leave their comfort zone and give up the things they are used to, in order to allow new tastes, experiences, and people into their lives.
- They have a strategy on how to deal with crisis, cravings, or self-doubts.

- They are not afraid to stand up for what they believe in and are prepared to explain, but also defend, their way of life without confrontation.
- They prepare and eat their food mindfully.

So, how do you apply mindfulness to anger management?

While some therapists recommend controlling anger—by counting to 10, or by hitting a pillow—others disagree with this approach as they believe this only heals the wound on the surface, while deep inside, it continues to fester. Instead, they recommend addressing the real problem behind the angry outburst, not the anger itself.

Regardless of their approach to anger management, more and more therapists recommend replacing traditional anger management techniques with mindfulness techniques.

Mindfulness is a very personal experience and there are many different ways of doing it, but, you can apply these steps to almost any activity or any situation.

7 basic steps to mindfulness:

1. Find a quiet spot to sit down and relax.
2. Set a time limit, like five to 10 minutes.
3. Still your mind and if it wanders, bring it back.

4. Become aware of your body: notice how your knees feel, how warm or cold your feet are, how tense or relaxed your abdomen is, or if you have any pains or aches.

5. Become aware of the noises around you: try to guess which bird is making that particular noise, what's going on in the street, whose dog is barking.

6. Become aware of any unusual smells: a neighbor having a barbecue, your roommate making a cup of coffee, the scent of lilac in the garden.

7. Slowly come back.

Day 16

Meditation

Numerous studies confirm that meditating for just 20 minutes a day, every day, can have numerous positive effects on both physical and mental health. This is largely because meditation relaxes the mind, which in turn reduces anger and anxiety, lowers blood pressure, and helps you feel grounded.

For those who practice it regularly, meditation can become a way of life. It can also help you come face to face with the feelings you keep hidden from others—or yourself. In the case of those who've suffered trauma or some kind of emotional or physical abuse, meditation can bring healing from the pain, shame, or guilt that is often present. This type of healing is particularly effective if you carry a lot of old, repressed anger.

Meditation is a skill, which means it can be taught and perfected with practice. There are many different ways to do it, and you can choose the style that suits you most based on what you want to achieve with it (e.g., calming vs. insight meditation), or which tradition, culture, or spiritual discipline you want to follow.

Of the dozens of types of meditation practiced today, the most popular ones are guided or unguided meditation, walking meditation, Buddhist meditation, Transcendental meditation, and meditation for sleep, for stress, for anger, for compassion.

The point is, there is no right or wrong way to meditate. Meditation is a very personal experience, and you should choose the one that works for you.

Where to Meditate

Meditation does not have to be a complicated affair, with a special practice space, dimmed lights, and uplifting music. Ideally, it should be practiced in a space dedicated to that purpose, however, that is optional.

Some people go to great lengths to create special effects in the meditation room, but these help only in the sense that they create an atmosphere in which it becomes easier to switch off and relax, and are in no way essential for successful meditation. With practice, you can learn to slip into a meditative state anywhere, regardless of the external and internal "noise."

3 things to bear in mind when creating a meditation space at home:

- **Find a space**

    Very few of us can set aside an entire room for meditation, so meditation space is usually a corner of a room which has another purpose, like a bedroom or a study. The meditation space can also be a table decorated for that purpose, a bookshelf, or even a tree trunk or a bench in the garden.

- **Decorate the space**

   This is what will make it conducive to meditation. As meditation is a very personal experience, anything that helps you enter a meditative state is fine—a statue of Buddha, unusual pieces of rock or wood, crystals, candles, photographs, flowers, dry leaves, fruits.

- **Make your space sacred, i.e. special**

   You make your meditation space sacred by making it look and "feel" special compared to other parts of your living space. This is why you should never keep "mundane" things in it, like books, magazines, food, or clothes.

Health Benefits of Meditation

While, for most people, meditation is a relaxation process, in Ayurveda, it's a detoxifying one—it helps clear "waste" products from the mind. It revolves around training your mind to focus and release negative mental energy that affects your thoughts, emotions, and behavior.

Meditation affects all aspects of our being:

- On an emotional level, it's an effective tool for beating stress, depression, and anxiety.

- On a mental level, it helps still your inner chatter so you can concentrate and relax more easily while ignoring distracting thoughts.

- On a physical level, it calms you down. When your heartbeat slows and blood pressure drops, your brain produces alpha, instead of beta waves. After spending some time in this relaxed but alert alpha state, you'll feel as refreshed as if you've had a nap.

Numerous studies show that regular meditators are generally healthier than non-meditators, and that meditation helps not only with stress-related disorders but with many other modern-day diseases like migraines, irritable bowel syndrome, asthma, anxiety, mild depression, high blood pressure, and heart disease.

Meditation techniques

Meditation is about stilling your mind and emptying it of distracting thoughts. It's best if you can meditate at the same time and place every day. How long you do it for is unimportant, as long as you do it properly. If you are new to meditation, start with 10 minutes a day, and by the end of the week, you should start to notice improvements.

Basic meditation technique:

1. Sit comfortably—either in the lotus position or, if your back is weak, in a straight-backed chair with your feet on the floor.

2. Close your eyes. Calm down.

3. Breathe slowly and steadily.

4. To keep yourself focused, you can repeat a mantra and gaze at a *mandala* or a candle flame. This is optional.

5. When you have finished, slowly open your eyes, move your arms and legs to encourage circulation, then stand up. Have a glass of water to ground yourself, as some people feel dizzy after sitting still for a long time.

Types of Meditation

The type of meditation you choose to do should be the one that works for you and should address the reason you are doing it—to calm down, to gain spiritual insight, to sleep better, and so on.

Meditation for stress and anxiety

Life is stressful as is, but if your day starts with traffic-induced stress and ends the same way—especially if you spend long hours getting to and from work—this can quickly become too much.

The reason consistent, daily meditation is so effective for stress-management is that it helps you reprogram your brain so it becomes less reactive and more responsive.

Stress usually makes people worry too much, and the racing thoughts make it difficult to focus on anything. Meditation is a very useful tool to quiet an overactive mind. With regular practice, you can learn how to detach yourself from the endless thoughts—not by forgetting about them, but by controlling how much you stay with them.

Meditation for anger

While there are different forms of meditation to choose from, the so-called "anger meditation" is aimed at addressing your anger problem not by controlling your anger, but by letting it run its course.

To this effect, meditation helps shift your focus from thinking about who or what made you angry to the actual feeling of anger. Feel the rage, embarrassment, frustration, or whatever other emotions your anger provokes. If there is a part of your body that is hot or burning with anger, like your face, stomach, or head, become aware of it.

Focus on that spot, and start breathing slowly and deeply. Try to bring your breath to that area. Keep going until you can feel the negative energy dissolve.

Meditation for sleep

This type of meditation teaches you not to get caught up in negative thoughts before going to bed. For many people, it isn't until they go to bed, or just before they do so, that they can finally slow down and relax. It is then that they start mulling over the day behind them or ahead of them. So, instead of getting themselves ready sleep by slowing down, they activate their mind by thinking about the various problems they have to deal with or the tasks awaiting them in the morning.

Meditation for sleep is usually a guided meditation that will help you let go of whatever you are thinking about until you become relaxed enough to fall asleep. This process revolves around the fact that meditation helps lower the heart rate and encourages slower breathing.

To help fight insomnia, don't think, read, or watch anything exciting that could start you thinking or worrying. Instead, focus on something calming and peaceful, like a photo, music, or thought, and watch your body wind down as it prepares for sleep.

Guided vs. unguided meditation

In guided meditation, you are led through meditation "moves" by a teacher who takes you through all the steps of a particular meditation technique and who suggests how you can apply what you've learned into your everyday life. This type of meditation is particularly good for beginners.

During unguided or silent meditation, you meditate on your own, either completely alone or as part of a group, and no one explains the process. This can be as simple as sitting quietly and concentrating on your breath while emptying your mind of distracting thoughts, or you can apply a particular meditation technique (like meditation for anger, sleep, and so on).

Zen meditation

Zen meditation focuses on breath and how it moves through your body. You think of nothing and let the mind "just be."

Anger Management

With this type of meditation, you cultivate both mindfulness and alertness.

Mantra meditation

With this type of meditation, instead of focusing on the breath to quiet the mind, you focus on a mantra. Your mantra could consist of a syllable, word, or a phrase which sums up what you believe in or what you aspire to.

The philosophy behind the mantra meditation is that the subtle vibrations associated with the repeated mantra can encourage positive change, boost self-confidence, reduce fear, and encourage empathy. Basically, a mantra should guide you in the way you want to live your life, so you choose a mantra that strikes a chord with you.

You can choose a quote:

- "Our greatest glory is not in never falling, but in rising every time we fall." (Confucius)
- "A person is what he or she thinks about all day long." (Ralph Waldo Emerson)
- "Opportunities don't happen, you create them." (Chris Groser)
- "They cannot take away your self-respect if you don't give it to them." (Mahatma Gandhi)

You can also create a personal mantra which sums up your goals and aspirations:

- I can and I will
- Live simply
- I write my destiny
- Seize the day

Transcendental meditation (TM)

TM is a silent mantra meditation, usually practiced for 20 minutes twice a day, although there are many variations. You meditate with your eyes closed and repeat a mantra assigned to you by your teacher. While you meditate this way, your thinking process "transcends" and is replaced by a state of pure consciousness.

Unlike other types of meditation, TM requires formal training by a certified teacher. It does not require concentration or contemplation, just breathing normally and focusing your attention on the mantra.

Some studies suggest that this type of meditation is not a good choice for those suffering from a certain psychiatric condition.

Walking meditation

During walking meditation, you are physically active and focused on the experience of walking. You walk very slowly and concentrate on your breath. Ideally, you should do this in a place where you will not be distracted by either people, traffic, or scenery.

You can practice barefoot or wear light shoes, and you can walk in a circle if you are doing this in a small garden. Try to be aware of the sounds around you and of yourself moving in that particular location. Walking meditation is a great technique for improving concentration.

The internationally-renowned self-help author and motivational speaker Wayne Dyer had great advice how life should be lived: "Become slower in your journey through life. Practice yoga and meditation if you suffer from 'hurry sickness.' Become more introspective by visiting quiet places such as churches, museums, mountains, and lakes. Give yourself permission to read at least one novel a month for pleasure."

Day 17

Zen Buddhism and the Importance of Living in the Present

What is perhaps the most striking difference between Zen Buddhism and Western culture is the understanding of happiness. While most people would define happiness as getting what they want—having a certain way of life or certain material possessions—Zen philosophy is based on the idea that we should stop expecting our lives to develop the way we think they should.

Unfortunately, the more we look for something to make us happy, the more likely we are to be disappointed. But for Buddhists, true happiness is a state of mind, and they look deep within when searching for it.

Zen tools that can help you reach a stage when you start looking for fulfillment within, rather than without, are meditation, mindfulness, and the practice of loving kindness.

Living according to these principles not only makes it easier to find your bliss, but makes it very difficult to develop any negative emotions—particularly anger.

What is Zen About?

While interest in Zen Buddhism is growing, many believe that following this philosophy is not possible in the 21st century. It's true that the modern world is very different from the time when Buddhism first appeared; however, the main obstacle to a Zen way of life is that obsession with material possessions, consumerism, and personal ambition—not spiritual development—have become the core values of Western culture.

Zen is about peaceful simplicity, but the stress of everyday life makes it difficult to aim for harmony within. Still, it's possible to embrace Zen values if you manage to slow down and live mindfully.

5 steps to adopting Zen philosophy amidst the chaos of modern life:

1. Find your meditation technique

Meditation is key for the Zen way of life, so choose how you want to do it. There are many styles to choose from, but the most important element of successful meditation is being focused. If you have a busy lifestyle and multitasking helps you cope, be prepared to give up that way of life. Your overall performance and results in anything you do will improve greatly if you start concentrating on one thing at a time.

2. Enjoy the moment

Learn to be content with who you are and what you have. When you learn to accept the life you are living, you stop worrying, and when you are free of worry you enjoy life more. Savoring every moment amidst the stress and chaos we're drowning in is not easy, but it's the only way to keep life from passing you by.

The well-known Vietnamese Zen Monk Thich Nhat Hanh said it all: "Drink your tea slowly and reverently, as if it is the axis on which the world earth revolves slowly, evenly, without rushing toward the future."

3. Look for happiness within

Some people are happy wherever they are, while others are unhappy, regardless. It's pointless to look for happiness in far-off places, better-paid jobs, or faster cars. Happiness is wherever you are right now, because it is within you. Instead of searching for it far and wide, look deep within.

4. Do one thing at a time

Most people have to juggle family, career, and social life, so multitasking has become a way of life. However, when you live like this, all you are doing is shifting your focus from one thing to another throughout the day. When you are not fully focused, and instead trying to do several things at the same time, a lot of your energy and time is wasted. You achieve much more if you give your full attention to whatever you're doing, rather than hoping to get more things done by taking on multiple tasks.

5. Be kind to yourself and others

In some ways, Buddhism and emotional intelligence are based on the same values: understanding, empathy, and forgiveness. When you learn to forgive (both yourself and others), you stop judging and blaming. When you try to understand why someone has done something that upset you, you stop feeling angry. When you practice gratitude, you realize how good life actually is. Whatever you decide to do, don't underestimate the power of kindness.

Zen Approach to Anger

We all get angry from time to time, but we deal with this powerful emotion in different ways. Some cultures repress it, while others express it freely—some even enjoy the feeling.

From the Zen point of view, feeling angry is simply wasting your energy on a mental state which serves no purpose. Buddhists approach anger in a pragmatic way—while they don't deny it, they will do nothing to help it grow.

While psychologists tell us anger is normal and we should express it in a constructive way, in Buddhism, anger is seen as the most negative and destructive force—one which can easily destroy all the good in the world. So, they approach anger in a typically Buddhist way: by neutralizing it with non-anger.

5 Zen things to do when you start getting angry:

1. It's OK to be angry, don't deny it

To Buddhists, fear and anger are energy-draining emotions which can control your life if you let them. With patience and practice, you can learn to avoid these mental states.

2. Learn how not to get angry

In Buddhism, anger gets a bad reputation—mainly because it revolves around ego. Still, Buddhists believe in practicing loving kindness even with those who make them angry. Buddhists don't behave aggressively when angry, nor do they try to suppress anger. They deal with it by observing it, but not participating in it. In other words, they neutralize it with understanding and compassion.

3. Cultivate patience

If you can't help feeling angry, give yourself time to calm down so you can communicate without making a scene or causing harm. Acknowledge the anger and embrace it. Wait. Given enough time, and your anger will vanish on its own. Patience gives you the chance to analyze your angry feelings and understand why you feel a certain way.

4. Don't feed anger

While some therapists recommend venting your anger in a way that will not cause harm, like pounding on a pillow, Buddhists believe that when you express your anger, either verbally or physically, you help it grow. When you ignore it, though, you starve it.

5. Compassion takes courage

Many people feel strong when they are angry, probably because of the adrenaline rush that floods the brain, and regard those who never show anger as weak cowards. In Buddhism, it's the other way around.

Buddhists believe showing anger is a sign of weakness, while having the strength to acknowledge anger, or the fear you feel when facing an angry person or when in a dangerous situation, is a sign of real strength.

Like most Eastern philosophies, Zen Buddhism teachings focus on acceptance and patience. Zen teaches us to be observant of what's going on around us and to embrace both the good and the bad, for there is a reason for everything.

As Robert Green pointed out, "Everything that happens to you is a form of instruction if you pay attention."

Day 18

Inner Peace Techniques for Anger Management

None of us go through life unscathed and, over time, we all devise various coping strategies to help us deal with stress, problems, anger, and disappointments. However, not all coping strategies are healthy.

The unhealthy coping strategies are what most people typically fall back on, mainly because these require the least effort and offer instant gratification. Unfortunately, they often have long-term negative effects on our health. These strategies include alcohol, drugs, antidepressants, smoking, and comfort eating.

On the other hand, healthy coping strategies, which offer a better long-term solution, are not always easy to implement and it may take quite some time for the first improvements to show.

Healthy anger management strategies are based on techniques which help you take control of your emotions and minimize the effects of angry outbursts. Eastern philosophies, such as Buddhism, Taoism, and Yoga, recommend gentle, yet powerful and effective, ways of managing anger that focus on inner peace and self-discipline.

The Tao of Inner Peace

Taoism is a belief system that promotes self-acceptance, inner peace, and flexibility. The reason Taoism and other Eastern philosophies have become so popular in the West is that as life becomes more complex and people find themselves facing overwhelming challenges on all levels, they try to find an alternative way of dealing with stress and restoring inner balance.

Taoism teaches many things, the most important of which is that the past is behind you and the future is not here yet—you should focus on the present moment. And this is why these ideas are so difficult for many to grasp. In the West, people spend their entire lives ruminating about their past mistakes and worrying about how they'll cope with the future. Being overwhelmed by uncertainty (because they constantly worry about the future) and mentally exhausted (from constantly thinking about what happened in the past) are the main reasons why anxiety, depression, and mental disorders are rising to epidemic proportions in the developed world.

Tao is big on forgiveness, so its approach to anger management is to forgive. Whether or not you forgive doesn't really matter, however, as it won't change what happened in the past. Which leads us to Taoism's key take on life—acceptance. Accept the past for what it is, because it's been and gone. Focus on the here and now.

Taoism is not a religion, but a belief system whose main doctrine is that only harmony within people can create harmony in the environment. It deals with anger by cultivating empathy, even for those who make practitioners angry. Through the constant search for inner peace, Taoists develop the ability to understand the suffering of others—even their enemies—without judgment.

<u>4 Taoist tips on achieving inner peace:</u>

Find your own happiness

People need different things to feel fulfilled. There is no recipe to finding happiness, because happiness means different things to different people. It's only when you find your own meaning in life that you will have found true happiness.

Peace is not around you—it's inside you

To reach a stage where you can find peace amidst crowds, noise, and chaos, you have to be able to switch off—regardless of what's going on around or inside you. This is achieved through meditation, which is a great tool for developing self-discipline.

Drop expectations

Expectations are a major cause of anger, because they make you over-ambitious, competitive, and frustrated. People are rarely satisfied with what they have and always want more. According to Taoism, the more you expect, the less you become: the key to happiness is to live in the present and practice gratitude.

Simplify your life

When you declutter your life and your mind from all the unnecessary things, thoughts, and information, you create space for the people and experiences that really matter.

Yoga

Despite the way many people approach yoga, it is much more than a workout. It's a spiritual tradition that brings together the body, mind, and spirit, and *asanas* are only a small part of it. According to yoga philosophy, the main purpose of physical exercises is to prepare the body for long periods of meditation, because you need to be mentally strong and physically flexible to be able to sit still for extended periods of time.

 inner balance. Its three main elements are *pranayama* (breathing exercises), meditation, and *asanas* (physical exercises). And this is where many people who do yoga get it wrong.

To most people (in the West, at least), yoga is merely a way of exercising their bodies. However, although these exercises have proven health benefits, that's not what yoga is really about. Without *pranayama*, ethical practices, and meditation, you are not really practicing yoga.

This means that if you can do only simple poses but understand and follow the philosophy of yoga, you are at a much higher level of yoga practice than someone who can do even the most demanding exercises without understanding why they are doing it.

There are many different schools of yoga, but they all revolve around balance in the mind and body. And, just like other spiritual traditions, yoga can teach us how to react to anger without repressing it or acting aggressively.

According to yoga philosophy, anger should be avoided at all costs because it undermines the very essence of yoga—achieving happiness and freedom.

The ancient yogis firmly believed in and practiced the mind-body approach to life. To them, anger was a kind of blockage at the mental, physical, or spiritual level. To free up the blocked energy, they used a combination of asanas, *pranayama*, and meditation techniques as main anger management tools with which they distracted the angry mind from the negative thoughts. The basic yoga model for controlling anger is to stop the inner chatter (with meditation) and shift the focus from the anger trigger to exercise and breathing (with *asanas* and *pranayama*).

These practices help with anger management by putting you in a mental state which promotes tranquility and boosts self-esteem while improving your physical health through balancing the production of hormones.

<u>3 ways yoga helps control your anger:</u>

1. **Yoga calms you down**

Meditation and breathing techniques are the essence of yoga. They help you stop the inner chatter—and once that happens, it's easier to feel relaxed and stress-free. Anyone who has attended a yoga class knows how light and calm they feel afterward. This is because yoga practice reduces stress hormones (cortisol and adrenaline) and induces the relaxation response (by raising levels of oxytocin, a hormone that reduces blood pressure and improves the levels of certain neurotransmitters that are usually low in those who are overwhelmed with negativity). And it is only in this relaxed state of mind that we can clearly "see" the real reason for our anger or anxiety and come to terms with it. So, there is science-based evidence that yoga practice starts a number of positive chemical changes within your body.

2. Yoga boosts your confidence

Doing yoga helps build your physical and mental strength, which in turn boosts how you feel about yourself and your body. As your body becomes more supple, your skin more radiant, and you begin to walk more gracefully, you can't but feel proud of yourself. Another reason your confidence soars is that yoga improves your health on both the physical and mental levels, which indirectly affects how you feel about yourself and your life.

3. Yoga unblocks your energy

Yoga is all about the balance of the body, mind, and soul. For this to happen, the energy within your body has to flow freely. Unfortunately, it is often blocked due to prolonged stress, chronic fatigue, repressed emotions, fear, or depression. As a result, emotions can become unbalanced, and you may easily become overwhelmed with negativity. When energy "flows" freely, so do your emotions, and healthy emotions produce healthy thoughts.

There are several asanas that are particularly powerful when used for the release of pent up anger and frustration, and *garbhasana* and *koormasana* are believed to be the most eficient ones.

According to the well-known yoga teacher and author, TKV Desikachar, "The success of yoga does not lie in the ability to perform postures but in how it positively changes the way we live our lives and our relationships."

Day 19

Cognitive Behavioral Therapy

Anger can have many triggers and, depending on one's temperament, culture, and level of emotional intelligence, can be a positive or a destructive force. We start learning about anger management from the moment we are born: babies cry with anger if they are left hungry or wet; some children throw tantrums if they can't get what they want, while others try to get the same thing by being nice and sweet; and as adults, we learn to deal with frustrations almost on a daily basis.

However, when we find ourselves in situations that are far too complex to be resolved on our own, or when faced with mental health disorders which require a professional approach, it's best to seek a good therapist.

Anger Management Counseling

Counseling works for many mental disorders, including anger management. While there are many different approaches to this problem, perhaps best-known is cognitive-behavioral therapy (CBT). The best thing about it is that you can achieve considerable improvements relatively quickly, in about two months.

CBT's approach to anger management is to address a combination of situations and beliefs which may have contributed to how you feel about yourself, as well as to the reasons when and why you experience anger. It focuses mainly on your childhood experiences and treatment, including the beliefs you were fed with and whether you were mistreated or belittled.

However, there are many other types of therapy, and the anger symptoms you are experiencing may help you decide which one would be the best for you.

3 types of anger symptoms:

1. **Physiological** (rapid heart rate, shaking, aggression towards others, etc.)
2. **Cognitive** (difficulties concentrating or remembering, dreaming of revenge, etc.)
3. **Behavioral** (arguments which result in violence, reckless driving, alcohol abuse, etc.)

People struggling with mental disorders often struggle to determine which therapy would work best for them. With so many options to choose from, it's perhaps best to consult your doctor for advice on this. Still, you should also familiarize yourself with what each therapy consists of, for there may be some that would suit you more.

Different anger management therapies:

- **In-person therapy**

    This is when you see a therapist on a regular basis

over an extended period of time. It can be over the phone or online, in a group or on a one-to-one basis.

- **Online counseling**

    This is a relatively new type of counseling and requires you to have a computer or a smartphone. For many, it offers an original and innovative method of treatment. Although this type of therapy would save you a lot of time, it may not suit those who prefer face-to-face interaction or lack IT skills.

- **Group therapy**

    The best thing about this kind of therapy is that it provides both a therapist and a support group. This type of counseling is often preferred by those who enjoy being part of a group and don't mind discussing their problems in front of other people. They also stand to benefit from listening to what sort of problems others may be facing and how they cope with them.

- **Residential anger management**

    This type of therapy is more intense and is used for people whose lives have been severely affected by their inability to deal with anger. On the upside, clients are away from their everyday life and can focus completely on the therapy, but this kind of treatment takes a lot of commitment, and not everyone is able to be away from their job or families for an extended period of time.

Another option is to treat anger management with medication, which usually involves antidepressants, mood stabilizers, or antipsychotic drugs.

Medication is prescribed to patients with severe anger problems, but usually only as a short-term solution until they have calmed down and can start therapy. Drugs are generally avoided, as they often come with side effects and there is the possibility of addiction. For this reason, medication is usually recommended only as a temporary solution.

Cognitive Behavioral Therapy (CBT)

Cognitive behavioral therapy (CBT), which is successfully used for many different disorders, is based on the idea that the best way to stop the vicious cycle of negative thoughts, emotions, and behavior is to replace the destructive thought patterns with positive ones.

CBT is very effective in anger management and focuses on teaching patients both how to control their thoughts and emotions and how to interpret them in a positive way.

7 steps of anger management with CBT:

1. **Avoid negative thoughts**

Those who are always negative about life will never be able to see anything positive around them. If your mind is overwhelmed with negativity, you need to learn to look at life from a different angle and realize that things are not as bad as you may have thought.

CBT is about looking at the world, and your life, with more objectivity, and realizing how much your negative thoughts "color" your experiences. When you learn to change the way you react to situations which provoke negative emotions, you will know that your anger management therapy has succeeded. For example, stop feeling that jokes about overweight people are always aimed at you, stop beating yourself up for not having done more for your grandparents while they were alive, or focus on improving your performance instead of worrying you might lose your job.

Your thoughts affect your feelings, and vice versa—a negative thought pattern eventually turns to anger or self-anger. You don't have to have happy thoughts all the time, but neither should you focus only on thoughts which make you fearful, anxious, or angry. It's not a cliché that a positive state of mind creates opportunities and attracts positive experiences.

2. **Identify where your anger is coming from**

The main aim of CBT therapy is to get patients to understand what initiates the cycle of negative thoughts, and to learn to avoid them or stop them before they get out of hand. Almost anything can be a trigger to a negative emotion, but it's the way you react to a trigger that decides whether it turns into a negative thought or behavior, or whether you simply register it and let it go.

Get into the habit of analyzing your anger. Is there a pattern? Is it getting worse? How often does it happen? Are triggers always the same? If you know where your anger is coming from, you can either avoid the triggers or be mentally prepared to face them.

It's the way you interpret a thought, a memory, a comment someone makes, or an event that either improves or clouds your judgment. This is why negative self-talk can be so destructive.

3. **Cultivate a nurturing environment**

People in your environment can be a pillar of comfort and support or a cause of constant sabotage. They can help pick you up when you're down, or make you feel even worse about yourself than you already do. This is why choosing your company is so important, especially if you are oversensitive and tend to take things personally, or have a problem controlling your temper. If your reaction is easily triggered, and especially if you have a history of violence, you should try to surround yourself with people who are least likely to push your buttons.

This is not always possible, but what is possible is for you to make some changes in your behavior or daily routine to better avoid situations which make you angry. For example, if you have a problem with road rage, consider taking public transport or finding an alternative route to work. If you have a problem with certain individuals, try to get them to meet you on neutral ground, like in a coffee shop or a park, rather than at their office or home, where being on their "territory" may make you feel more vulnerable and less in control of your emotions.

4. **Respond quickly to negative emotions**

How quickly you react to a negative thought will decide how successful you are in preventing that thought from becoming a thought pattern. Negativity breeds negativity, so the trick is to prevent a negative thought from becoming a negative emotion, which can become a negative reaction.

5. **Learn to identify your threshold**

Sometimes, a change of scene is all it takes for anger to subside. This could mean walking away from your office for a few moments, from your flat for a couple of hours, or moving away from your parents' home. Many conflicts happen as a result of a lack of "breathing space," so when you feel you're beginning to get angry, if possible, remove yourself from that environment for a while.

Some people can quickly come up with ideas about how to respond to an anger trigger, others need more time to think about how to react. Although it's not possible to walk away in the middle of an important meeting or a job interview, when you feel anger rising, at least take a couple of moments to compose yourself. Simply, count to ten or take a few deep breaths before responding.

6. **Weaken your triggers if you can't prevent them**

Learn how to think rationally so you can calm yourself down when under stress and don't take it out on others. A negative thought allowed to get out of hand can lead to rage which is often targeted at those who happen to be around, even if they have nothing to do with your problem.

If avoiding a trigger fails to work, at least try to weaken it by developing a positive thought or repeating a positive affirmation which will counter the negative thought that makes you angry—if you think you are not popular, think of those who actually enjoy spending time with you; if you're angry with yourself for being overweight, think of all those people who were once overweight, and managed to get fit through their own efforts.

If you feel very negative and nothing seems to make it better, try doing something drastic. First of all, leave the place where the negative thought happened, and avoid reading or watching any negative material (like news dealing with war, terrorism, or the destructive effects of climate change). Don't talk to those who are always complaining, sad, or depressed. Although watching news can serve as a distraction from your negative thoughts, it can also make them worse. Fear-provoking news, movies, or sermons will only feed your negativity, while what you need to do is starve it of energy.

7. Improve communication skills

Lack of communication is very often the main cause of misunderstandings, arguments, or angry scenes. When you learn to communicate effectively and know how to express your feelings, you will see that many of the situations which make you angry will disappear. Most people prefer talking to listening and, very often, this is where the problem lies. For example, if you had listened carefully, you would have understood what the client really wanted, or if you let your friends know how much it upsets you when they mention your acne problem, you wouldn't end up angry and hurt every time someone brings this up.

8. Challenge your thinking

It's not easy to admit you were wrong. After you have identified your anger triggers, ask yourself if perhaps there may be other reasons for your anger which the triggers have masked? What if what you think someone meant is not true? Is there another way to think about the incident that provoked such a violent reaction in you? Challenging yourself takes courage and maturity, but you'll be surprised what you can find if you dig deep enough.

A negative mindset is never the result of a single negative thought. It is the consequence of a series of negative thoughts which you have lived with for some time—maybe all your life. Be mindful of your environment, the people you socialize with, and the things you read and watch, as all that contributes to your state of mind.

Day 20

Nutrition for Stress Relief

Your diet is not only the fuel that keeps you going, it also affects how often you'll get sick, how quickly you'll recover, how much weight you'll gain, how long you'll live, and more.

There is a reason Hippocrates said, "Let thy food be thy medicine and thy medicine be thy food."

Diet does not only help maintain good health, it can also be used as a natural medicine to correct certain imbalances—more fiber will improve digestion, less unhealthy fats will reduce your chances of heart disease, less salt will lower your blood pressure, antioxidant-rich foods will lower your risk of cancer.

Mood-enhancing plants can be used to soothe a troubled mind and ease many psychological problems, and you don't have to be ill to reap these benefits. You can use them to lift your spirits, bring tranquility, calm down, achieve mental clarity, or aid meditation.

According to Ayurveda, combining foods of different colors is the best way to eat, but a new study reveals that this kind of diet is not only nutritious and physically healthy, but is also good for your mood—different colors carry different energies and these have a direct influence on your mood. Whether you are aware of it or not, color stimulates your emotions and motivates your decisions.

Fight Mental Disorders with Nutrition

Although we are all affected by stress, not everyone knows that it can be controlled with a diet. Certain foods provide natural protection from stress simply because they increase the levels of hormones in the body that naturally fight stress. As well, there are foods and beverages that reduce stress by lowering the levels of hormones that trigger them.

<u>7 foods that help you beat stress:</u>

1. **A warm drink**

    We all know that a cup of tea will calm you down, a cup of warm milk or cocoa before going to bed will help you sleep peacefully, and that a cup of soup helps if you're not feeling well. It's not so much the nutrients from these drinks that provide a sense of calm and healing, but the warmth of the beverage itself. For a number of reasons, there's something very comforting about a warm drink.

2. **Dark chocolate**

    As all chocolate lovers know, the taste and smell of chocolate alone are enough to reduce stress. Besides, dark chocolate is rich in antioxidants, which are known to fight stress as well as protect the body from free radicals. If taken daily, it can help you improve your heart health, lower the blood pressure, prevent some types of cancer, as well as produce endorphins which will improve your mood. If taking it daily, you shouldn't take more than 30 grams.

3. **Healthy Carbs**

Carbohydrates increase levels of serotonin, a chemical that boosts mood and reduces stress, which indirectly improves cognitive function. However, there are healthy and unhealthy carbs. To improve your mood and reduce stress-induced anger, include the following foods in your daily diet: sweet potato, brown rice, oats, quinoa, buckwheat, beetroots, beans, chickpeas, carrots, mangos, bananas, blueberries, and apples.

4. **Avocados**

Rich in omega-3 fatty acids, this is one of the healthiest fruits you can eat. These essential acids are known to reduce stress and anxiety, boost concentration, and improve mood.

5. **Fatty fish**

Another great source of omega-3 fatty acids, which not only beat stress but ease depression. The best source of omega-3 fatty acids are tuna, halibut, salmon, herring, mackerel, sardines, and lake trout.

6. **Nuts**

Nuts are full of vitamins and healthy fatty acids. They are particularly rich in vitamin B which neutralizes the effects of stress. Add almonds, pistachios, or walnuts to fruit or vegetable salads, muesli, yogurt, or soups.

7. **Vitamin C**

    High levels of vitamin C help reduce stress, so eat fresh fruit and vegetables or take supplements.

Our bodies respond to threatening situations by sending signals to the brain that it's in trouble. The brain reacts by requiring food that will help it think more clearly and be ready for a physical response—fight or flight.

The main threat we face today is that of prolonged stress, which our bodies react to in the same way as when confronted with physical danger. However, after the threat has passed or after you've escaped, your body goes into a recovery mode characterized by an increased appetite to recover from the shock and exhaustion. It is at this stage that many people reach for comfort foods to calm down and recover the energy lost during a stressful situation.

This is how most of us fight stress. However, there is a healthier approach to stress-relief.

3 tips on how to manage stress with diet:

- On a stressful day, eat less and more often.
- Eat plenty of fruits and vegetables to get the nutrients needed for fighting stress.

- Avoid or limit caffeine-rich foods, such as coffee, tea, soft drinks, and chocolate.

Nutrition and Anger Management

Anger behavior ranges from screaming into a pillow or going for a run all, all the way up to murder, and as many people with anger problems end up in jail, even mild anger outbursts should not be ignored—especially if they happen repeatedly. There are different ways of treating anger disorders, one of the easiest being with a healthy diet.

Studies suggest that uncontrollable outbursts of anger are only one of the many symptoms of various mood disorders, like depression, anxiety, insomnia, addiction, and so on. Interestingly, most such individuals have hypoglycemia—a sugar handling problem.

The reason hypoglycemia is common in chronically angry individuals is because such people are often exposed to unnaturally high levels of adrenaline. In stressful situations, when the brain anticipates energy starvation, it triggers the secretion of adrenaline.

When that happens, there is a rush of adrenaline to feed the brain, as well as activation of the fight/flight hormone. In such a state, people become either defensive or aggressive.

Fortunately, this problem can be solved without drugs through a hypoglycemic diet based on four simple rules:

1. Avoid sugar and sugar-rich foods
2. Eat high-protein foods (fish, eggs, chicken, beef)

3. Snack every three hours on complex carbohydrate foods, including whole grains, fruits, legumes, green vegetables, and starchy vegetables, to help with the slow release of glucose

4. Eat plenty of green vegetables and fresh fruits

5. Take supplements such as vitamin B-complex, vitamin C, vitamin D, and probiotics.

Those who follow a hypoglycemic diet quickly normalize their blood sugar levels and stress hormones adrenaline and cortisol, which are responsible for mood swings, depression, anxiety, alcoholism, and other mental disorders that often lead to angry outbursts.

More and more scientists believe that what we eat contributes to how angry we feel, and numerous studies show that a diet high in trans fatty acids is directly linked to increased aggression.

Trans fats are unhealthy fats found in the foods we enjoy the most—French fries, fried and battered foods, pies, margarine sticks, shortening, frostings, pancakes and waffles, ice cream, ground beef, processed meats, cookies and cakes, biscuits, crackers, frozen dinners, and canned chili.

Giving up your favorite foods is not easy and is best done gradually over a couple of months, otherwise you may not be able to cope with the cravings. However, if you're struggling with an anger problem and know that nutrient deficiency is a major cause of your behavioral abnormalities, switching to a healthy eating plan will make a significant improvement.

The reason processed foods are so bad for your health is that they are nothing more than empty calories, which not only lack nutrition but also contain a lot of unhealthy color and taste additives. Only with a healthy diet will your body be able to produce the chemicals and hormones it needs for clear thinking, healthy mood, and balanced emotions.

In conclusion, you can keep your anger problem under control without therapy if you change your diet and stick to it.

Try a mood-stabilizing diet for a month, and see how your behavior changes and your mood improves. As Bethenny Frankel pointed out, "Your diet is a bank account. Good food choices are a good investment."

Mood-stabilizing diet:

1. Mood-boosting foods: fruits and vegetables—the less processed, the better
2. Plenty of dopamine-building foods: fish, poultry, eggs, and leafy greens
3. Omega-3 rich foods to fight depression: fish, flaxseed, chia seeds, walnuts
4. Magnesium-rich foods to support sleep and relaxation: almonds, spinach, pumpkin seeds, sunflower seeds
5. Vitamin D-rich foods to prevent mood disorders: fatty fish, egg yolks, liver
6. Limit sugar

Day 21

Putting It All Together

The idea behind writing this book was to showcase how you can transform your life by taking control of your thoughts. And when you control your thoughts, you can better control your emotions and your behavior.

In the stressful time we live in, our patience and tolerance are often challenged. Stress typically leads to more stress, and mental health problems are often the result of this vicious circle.

Negativity is a common side effect of chronic stress, as is poor anger management. And the reason people develop a negative mindset is often not because they have a negative attitude to life, but because they are overwhelmed by stress and anxiety.

So, how do you break this circle of stress-negativity-more stress-anger-more stress-more-negativity? By understanding where all this negativity is coming from, and by acknowledging that many times it is not stress, but your own self-limiting thoughts that make you see everything in a negative light.

Unfortunately, becoming positive doesn't happen overnight, nor can it happen on its own. That's something that has to be worked on, and that usually includes making some big, life-changing decisions.

Remap Your Mind

In a culture obsessed with youth, beauty, and fitness, one is constantly reminded of what they should look like. As a result, we have a trillion-dollar health and wellness industry which cashes in on the idea that there is no reason we should not all have perfect bodies, beautiful white teeth, and flawless skin.

However, while taking care of your body is important for your well-being, it doesn't mean you should neglect the part that often stays well-hidden, sometimes even from you—your mind. And just because your emotions and thoughts cannot be seen, while your teeth, body, and hair can, doesn't mean they are any less important.

In the overpopulated, fast, and competitive world of ours, it's easy to reach a stage where you become so overwhelmed with life that you can no longer keep track of all the changes taking place around you. Your brain can only take so much—when it can no longer manage the overload, it may respond by developing a mental health disorder.

If you can't manage your thoughts and feelings, you start living on auto-pilot: barely keeping your head above water, struggling to deal with the stress, fear, and anger that your life seems to be full of. Is it surprising that mental disorders are spreading like wildfire? Some studies even suggest that poverty is not the main reason for the rise in recorded crime, but the real reason is the increasing number of stressors that people are just not coping with.

So, when you hit a low point in life—or even better, before you do—why not do something to prevent the emotions of anger, frustration, and sadness from taking over your life? Take responsibility for what you are going through, but don't give in to defeat.

If you can afford it, go on a mental makeover retreat. If you can't, you can turn over a new leaf by giving yourself a mental makeover without leaving the comfort of your home. Just like you can revamp your body, you can remap your mind with a new approach to life.

Mental Makeover

Mental makeover techniques are about successfully overcoming challenges, taking control of your emotions, and staying healthy and happy. They revolve around high self-esteem and a positive attitude.

10 tips on mental makeover:

1. **Know yourself**

   When you know yourself, you understand what situations make you feel uncomfortable and you avoid them when you can, or you come up with ways to deal with them in an emotionally-intelligent way. There is no recipe for happiness and contentment—it's good to understand what makes you happy so you can do more of it.

2. **Take control of your emotions**

   For good mental health, it's very important not to hold grudges or keep emotions bottled up. While the best way to let go of unexpressed emotions is to talk about them, if there are issues you don't feel like discussing or if you have no one to talk to, you can choose a non-verbal way of communication—writing, journaling, painting, singing, or dancing. The trick is to learn to express your emotions in a way that's not offensive to others or harmful to you.

3. **Keep your brain in shape**

   The reason the mind deteriorates so quickly once people go into retirement is that it's no longer stimulated. While you work, you are constantly under some kind of stress and pressure, and although this can be bad for your health, it keeps your mind alert.

   To prevent, or at least slow, mental deterioration, think of games or activities that would keep your brain occupied. If you lack company, get a pet. If you like reading, join a library. Go for lectures, do crosswords, play sports, join a club, learn a new language or skill. When you cultivate new interests, you open the door to new people and new experiences in your life.

4. **Learn to enjoy life**

   Why is this so hard? Some people feel uncomfortable, even guilty when they're enjoying themselves. Others don't know how to do it. Some feel it's a luxury they can't afford. Enjoying life is about finding pleasure in what you do, and it's not a luxury for it does not have to cost you anything.

Depending on your financial situation, it could be something as extravagant as an exotic vacation or as simple as meeting a friend for coffee, planting some flowers in your garden, or taking part in a dog show. Learning to enjoy life is about finding a way to feel happy, regardless of what you do or where you are. Enjoying life is about being happy to be alive.

5. Meditate

Meditation is a great way to still your mind and stop the inner chatter so you can "hear" the important stuff. Long-term daily meditation improves your health, and actually rewires your brain so you become calmer and better able to handle difficult situations. You also become more open-hearted and able to see things from others' points of view. In other words, you become more emotionally intelligent. It may sound like a cliché, but meditation does change people.

6. Cultivate mindfulness

If you embrace mindfulness as a way of life, you choose to be fully aware of your thoughts and emotions. The reason mindfulness is so important for your mental health is that it makes you feel "centered" and helps you cope with whatever life throws at you. It also improves your physical health by relieving stress, and can even reduce chronic pain. When you live mindfully, you are fully present in whatever situation you may find yourself.

7. **Focus on what you want, not on what you don't want**

One of the best ways to develop a positive mindset is to shift your mind from what you DON'T WANT and DON'T HAVE, and from what you CAN'T DO, to what you do want, have, and know. However, you have to approach this mindfully, because focus without intention gets you what you don't want.

8. **Healthy diet**

Food has a very real effect on our physical performance (by providing energy), mental activity (by providing mental clarity through vitamin- and antioxidant-rich foods), and emotions (by calming or alerting us, like chocolate, sugar, caffeine, tea). For long-term wellness, choose a diet that supports you on all levels of your being.

9. **Boost your self-image**

A true mental makeover is impossible if you struggle with low self-esteem. This is about how you think about yourself, what your appearance says about you, and how approachable you are. Without a positive self-image, you'll find it hard to get far in life. Perhaps the easiest way to improve your self-image is to think about yourself as you would like to be. As Napoleon Hill pointed out, "What the mind can conceive and believe, it can achieve."

10. Develop emotional intelligence

If your life is not too unbalanced, most of your mental blocks can be overcome by developing emotional intelligence skills, which you can learn from self-help books such as this one or from attending an emotional intelligence course. As an emotionally intelligent person, you will always be in touch with your inner world and rely on your self-awareness to guide you when making a decision.

Perhaps, the success of mental makeover depends on how much you believe in yourself. As Roy Bennett put it, "You are braver than you think, more talented than you know, and capable of more than you imagine."

Thank you

Before you go, I just wanted to say thank you for purchasing my book.

You could have picked from dozens of other books on the same topic, but you chose this one.

So, a HUGE thanks to you for getting this book and for reading all the way to the end.

Now, I wanted to ask you for a small favor. **Could you please consider posting a review on the platform? Reviews are one of the easiest ways to support the work of authors.**

This feedback will help me continue to write the type of books that will help you get the results you want. So, if you enjoyed it, please let me know.

Lastly, don't forget to grab a copy of your Free Bonus book *"Bulletproof Confidence Checklist."* If you want to learn how to overcome shyness and social anxiety and become more confident, then this book is for you.

 Just go to: https://theartofmastery.com/confidence/

www.ingramcontent.com/pod-product-compliance
Lightning Source LLC
LaVergne TN
LVHW052234110526
838202LV00095B/223